From the Mountaintop

POWERFUL MESSAGES OF INSPIRATION

From the Mountaintop

FRANCIA LA DUE

Radiant Books
New York

From the Mountaintop was originally published anonymously in 1914. Illustrated by Karem AHU. Mountain photos by Cathrine Langwagen and Burtn. Annotated by Radiant Books.

Illustrations © 2023 by Radiant Books
Annotations © 2023 by Radiant Books

Library of Congress Control Number: 2023950651

Published in 2023 by Radiant Books
radiantbooks.co

ISBN 978-1-63994-051-6 (hardback)
ISBN 978-1-63994-052-3 (paperback)
ISBN 978-1-63994-053-0 (e-book)

Dedicated to Humanity

BEHOLD!

I GIVE UNTO THEE A KEY

TABLE OF CONTENTS

Preface . . . . *xv*

To My Beloved 1
My Kingdom 2
Father Mine 2
What Doest Thou for Me? 3
Humanity 4
I — Thy Soul 5
I Stand and Wait 6
Be Merciful to God 7
The Face of Christ 7
My "Little Ones" 8
The Deliverer 8
The Heart of a World 9
The Wheel of Time 10
Spiritual Birth 11
Thou Wanderer 11
The Homage of the Heart 12
To the Neophyte 13
Thy Star and Mine 15
Renunciation 15
The Birth of the Soul 16
The Fruit of the Tree 16
Children of Light 17
The Earthborn God 17
The Wine of Life 18
The Guerdon of Humility 18
The Love Divine 19
The Bird of Life 19
The Armor of Faith 20
Love's Conquest 20
The Path of Duty 21
Life's Opportunities 21
The Harp of Infinity 21

As Ye Sow	22
The Soul of Song	22
The Goal	22
Mystery of Mysteries	23
Wing Thy Heart Home	23
The Child of Love	23
God's Thought	24
Love's Abode	24
The Tail of the Dragon	25
Rouse Ye!	25
Which of the Three?	26
Love the Avenger	27
Look Deep	28
God Still Lives	28
The Light of Peace	29
Come Forth!	29
A New Cycle	29
The Angel of Healing	30
Man	30
Veils of the Soul	31
Lift Up Your Heads	31
Come Back	33
Pride	33
Enter the Path	33
The Holy Flame	34
Cross and Crown	34
The Light of Life	35
A Prophecy	35
Hold, and Listen	36
Christ or Judas?	37
The God of Pain	38
The King Cometh	38
The Holy Angel, Love	39
Make Clean Thine Heart	39
Thy Heritage	41
The Draught of Lethe	41

The Place of Peace	41
The Path	42
To the Dead in Life	42
Compassion	43
The Cross of Fire	43
Thine Own	44
Illusion's Flames	44
The Soul's Opportunity	44
The Voice of God	45
Jewels of Light	45
Love and Hatred	45
Where Is God?	46
The Path Is Hard	46
Stand Up	47
The Gift of God	49
The Book	49
The Heights of Life	51
Find the Good	51
The Call of the Flesh	52
Give Way	53
The Gift of Life	53
Thy Crown	54
The Power to Build	54
No Recall	55
The Trimurti	55
The Dead in Life	56
The Price of Love	56
Justice Reigns	57
Listen	58
Thus Saith the Lord	58
The Christ-Born	59
Thy Trust	59
The Workshop	60
The Intervals of Life	63
"I Have Kept the Faith"	63
Open Thine Eyes	66

The Living Christ	67
Justice	67
"My Father"	68
The Weapons of the Self-Born	69
The Greatest Is Charity	70
To Mine Own	71
Prayer	72
Friendship	73
Hearken To Me	74
Lift Up Thine Eyes	74
The Guerdon or the Loss	75
Sing Soft and Low	75
The Latch	76
Thou Hast Done Well	77
The Central Flame	79
Faithfulness	79
Search	80
"He Comes"	80
Life in Death	81
Compassion's Veil	81
Shift Thy Load	82
Debtors to Life	82
The Speech of Christ	83
Loyalty	83
Ask Each Day	86
Look Within	86
The Northern Windows	86
Darkness	87
Make Room for Me	87
The Shadow	88
Answer Me	88
Endurance	89
The Scoffer	89
The Stricken Soul	90
Let Go	90
It	91

The Threefold Warning	93
The Peace of God	93
The Temple Plan	94
The Grave of Sin	94
Ye Too	94
Opportunity	95
The Diamond Soul	95
The Rich	96
Birds of Prey	96
Sorrow	97
The Highway	97
Truth	98
From God to Man	99
The Heart of God	99
Hold High Thy Trust	99
Thy Golden Opportunity	100
Grow Wings and Fly High	100
The Word Eternal	101
New Births	103
Will Divine	103
Seek the Cause	103
The Veil	104
The Perfect One	105
The Common Chord	105
The Light Within	105
The Web	106
Death	106
Fear	107
The Unfinished	108
The Right to Seek	108
Emotion	109
Thy Choice	110
Love's Offices	111
The World Pain	112
The Next Step	113
The Obstruction	114

The Nine Steps	114
The Stream of Sacrifice	115
The Need of Pain	115
The Stones of Sacrifice	116
The Victor	116
Your Hours	117
The Cyclic Rounds	117
The Umbilicus	118
Life's Demand	118
The Crown	119
Just So Far	119
The Father's Care	120
The Load	121
Wouldst Thou Win?	121
The Feast	123
Thy Bonds	123
Your Responsibility	124
Life Knots	124
Fulfillment by Faith	124
My Gifts to Thee	125
Cause and Effect	125
The Great Moment	126
Come	126
The Beautiful Message	127
His Birthright	127
Love Is God	129
Come Forth Thou Christ	129
The Song of Life	130
The Message	131
The Task	132
The Little Things	133
The Price	133
The Power of Loving	134
Twilight and Dawn	135
You Must Choose	136
The Will to Live	137

Loose Him	138
The Milestones	139
The Peace of All Fulfillments	140
Your Defeats	141
The Soul Redeemed	141
Light of the Soul	142
To the World	142
Lift Thou Thine Eyes to God	143
The Eternal Warfare	143
The Wheel of Suffering	144
The Pain of Progress	145
The Garden of the Soul	145
Relight Thy Torch	147
Life's Shine and Shadow	147
The Angel of the Path	148
The Lens of the Soul	148
The Law Fulfilled	149
Judge Not	149
Unselfish Love	149
The Inner Temple	150
Cease, and Sing	150
A Clarion Call	151
Warriors of Light	152
About the Author	*155*

PREFACE

Truth is its own authority; the light within alone is able to recognize the light without in any message, teachings, or teacher. Thus the Divine in the human recognizes and realizes its identity with the Divinity cased in human vestments — for Truth and that Divinity are akin — are one in fact.

On the Scroll of Infinite Duration is written in letters of flaming life, the basic meaning of the first Great Word — that Word which all evolving life is spelling out in orderly sequence, letter by letter, syllable by syllable, as the ages pass. The higher consciousness of the human soul is part of that scroll of light, and on that plane understands its Unity with All — but, entombed in matter and outer husks, the personal entity, though "trailing clouds of glory from afar" is seethed in oblivion and forgetfulness, so far as its real nature, its inherent divinity, is concerned.

Wars, pestilence, famines and cataclysms, with their attendant shocks of suffering serve to awaken the latent spiritual memories of man to the fundamental moral meaning of existence by stilling the outer self and driving it in, and for those "whose vision is single," vibrations of sound and light come from heights where stand the Sentinels of Life ever transmitting and modifying the cosmic evolutionary forces to the status and understanding of races and worlds on the levels below. Gently but persistently descend those cosmic vibrations into the valleys where dwell the multitudes. Ever and anon, the inner ear, sight or feeling, of some one in those valleys may catch a tinkle of sound, or sense a flash of light, or a color of cosmic feeling, falling from those altitudes celestial, and then — translated into terms of human understanding — a new keynote, a higher impulse, is given to human endeavor with deeper concepts of life; or it may give a more basic understanding of the true philosophy of Being; it may mean an uplifting poem or work of art, a high musical inspiration, a new scientific truth or invention that will further unify the races of the earth, or, in the field of politics and government be rendered into terms of a regenerating principle and plan for action that will move the world a step nearer that economic freedom in line with life's fundamental purpose.

Eternally beating, ever beating, the rain of spiritual influences fall ceaselessly on humanity, refreshing, quickening and awakening the human more and more to his interdependent greatness, spiritually, morally and materially, with all that is. Standing on life's peaks of snowy whiteness, where one may look down — and understand, the Word thunders its truth to the Inner Self and senses. In the valleys, however, are but the faint whisperings of that truth, not easily heard, and most easily misunderstood, yet the basic meaning of that Word of Life is attainable to all who unselfishly aspire — and search.

TO MY BELOVED

Arouse ye! Arouse ye, Children of the New Covenant! Why stand ye in the public places idle throughout the busy day? The war of the ages is upon thee — the strife between the Sons of Universal Light and the Brothers of the Shadow. The long list of the Sons of Betrayal, the Judas power of the accumulated ages, hath its arms about thy neck and is pressing upon thy cheek the kiss that bringeth crucifixion.

Awake, thou that sleepest, and the Logos[1] shall shine upon thee. The Christ in thine own soul whispers: "Be of good courage, I have overcome the world." The days of preparation are upon thee. Gird on that armor of Righteousness which is the heritage of every Son of the Living God, and strike for the freedom of the races of the earth from the clutch of the Beast, the embodied Mammon[2] who now holdeth in subjection the children of Man.

Think ye that no protest rises to the seventh heaven from the murdered Abels[3] of the long past ages? Think ye the Law hath lost its power because its judgments tarry long? Become one with the law. Enter thou the Holy of Holies with unsandaled feet and uncovered head, that the forces of Love, Law and Life may flow unobstructed through the Stone of Sacrifice upon which thou standest, and the return wave bear to thee the spiritual essence that shall make thee free. In freedom lies thy strength.

The sword of the Spirit shall be thy reward, and He whom thou lovest shall lead thee to living waters, for He is the Warrior of Light, the *Unconquerable*, for whom the hour shall never strike. He is thine own true Self, and when thy shadows flee away thou shalt behold the King in His beauty and holiness.

---

[1] *Logos* (*Greek*, "word") — the manifested Deity; the outward expression, or effect, of the cause which is ever concealed; a name or title of Jesus Christ.

[2] *Mammon* (*Aramaic*, "riches") — a term derived from biblical texts, representing material wealth or worldly possessions and often associated with greed and the pursuit of wealth as an ultimate goal.

[3] *Abel* — the second son of Adam and Eve, murdered by his brother Cain (see Genesis 4:1–8).

MY KINGDOM

I BUILT me a nest; I, Hamsa[1] — in the heart of a ball of fire. I brought from far-off regions of space huge relics of long dead spheres to build it strong and true to the lines Infinity fashions and bounds all living things. I lined it with coral reefs and with precious gems, wrought by the fiery lives; I brought fleecy clouds from the sky to soften and cool the glowing stones to which my nest must cling, lest the Storm-Gods, angered by my presumption, should tear it apart from its foundations and scatter its fragments afar.

Then I sat me down and waited in the solitudes of Time. Waited, till the whirling balls in the sky above had burst and scattered their glowing earthy embers on the surface of my nesting place and hemmed me in, close, warm, safe from the baffled fury of the Storm-Kings.

I brought forth my young; creeping things, plants, birds, fishes, animals, and finally man. Then I raised my wings and soared away to the heavens above.

Now I fly in never ceasing motion around my nesting place, watching, ever watching for the day to dawn when those I brought to birth and gave the chance to win the heritage of the blest, shall look up and see me, and seeing, shall know me as I am. Not as those that hate me, know me, but as I *am* in truth, to lover, friend and husband, bride and mother; and, having known me, yield themselves to me in love, that so at last I come into *my own*, my Kingdom, that I loved to life, long ages since.

FATHER MINE

FATHER mine! Though Thou hast cast me down where deep calls unto deep across the span of human woe, though Thou hast stripped from me the mantle of protection Thou gavest me, and left me naked, lone, exposed to every blast; though Thou

---

[1] *Hamsa* (*Sanskrit*, "swan") — a mystical bird, often identified with the Supreme Spirit in Hinduism.

hast given power unto mine enemy to raze my home and send its beams and rafters crashing down upon my shrinking form; yet I behold Thine everlasting, all-encircling arm outstretched to me, and through the storms and wreckage of my outer life I see the Star, the symbol of Thy Power, that evermore must rise and set upon Thy breast — the Star of Thy Nativity — and know that even as its rays reach out and lighten all the vaults of heaven, so doth a single ray of that same Star reach out and pierce the gloom within my heart and make a nesting place of light therein.

A single ray, but even so a carrier of the voice of God; a God that speaks such words as no mere human ear can bear, yet speaks in tones my soul doth understand, and says: "Fear not, for I am with thee in the dark as well as in the light, and I will cover thee with mine own hand and keep thee safe against the day when thy betrayer seeks the light of that fair star upon my breast which leads to thee. For not until thine enemy doth seek thee out and bind the bruises made upon thy tender flesh, and with repentance and rejoicing brings thee back unto thine own, can e'en a glimmer of that light fall o'er his blinded eyes."

He who doth strike his brother down and leave him to the beasts of prey, may never find his Father's house again, till led by that same brother's hand back to his Father's feet.

WHAT DOEST THOU FOR ME?

WHEN Star struck Star and space was quivering from the shock; while flames were flashing red and white-hot metals crept in streams between the fiery tongues which leaped from place to place in search of food for burning; I sought and found and held thee in the hollow of my hand till once again the power of Water intervened and cooled the molten mass; then gathered up the remnants and formed another ball on which my feet might rest the while I built another nesting place for thee.

Another day of time, when floods were loosed and overwhelmed the earth, on torrents fierce I rode to rescue thee. In crest, in trough of wave I sought and found and tore thee from the water demons' clutch, those demons of the depths who seize and drag the sons of men down to the ocean's floor and take their blood for starring gems to deck satanic crowns.

While other Gods looked down on earth from other suns in search of portents for their guidance in the war of worlds, I sought thee out *for* thou wert more to me than all dead worlds.

Through all the kingdoms of the earth, in war or peace, through blackest night and light of day, in this, another age, I sought thee in thy wanderings, paid thy ransom, brought thee home. And thou, what doest thou for me?

Thou now hast come unto the parting of the ways and if thou turnest from the way marked out by me and mine, then transient life alone remains for thee.

HUMANITY

AS SHINE the stars set in my kingly crown, the crown which my desire hath welded of my conquest of the Dragon of Illusion, and studded with the jewels of thy sacrifice, so shalt thou, the prince, the heir to all my universe of riches, shine in that great day when all mine own shall come to me to feast with me on viands all the ages gone have grown from seed sown in my body and watered by my deep compassion.

As vast as is my kingdom, even so is vast the love which sheltered and protected, conceived and bore thee, son of mine — the fiery essence of that love which clothes thee, as thou art clothed, with woven garment, clinging close about thy form — the love that all the waters of the misty deeps can never quench; the love which grows, like to the tree of life whose topmost branches touch the skies, with every day of every age that thou hast passed in battle with the powers of Hell.

Then canst thou doubt my purpose, scorn my messenger when every tree and flower and living thing points all unerringly to thought for thee, or strive to find some other way to reach the rest and bliss thy soul desires?

The poignant grief, the agony of spirit rising like the ocean's waves within thy heart, drawing from thy tensioned lips the cry "My Father," paves the way and floods the milestones with a light supernal, that thou shalt not be hindered when thy face is turned towards me, thy back upon the fleshly things that strew thy way and stay thy feet.

Yea, even more, for thou shalt *be* my crown, my *kingdom* and *my all*. Lo, I shall live in thee, as thou in me, when dawns that other day.

I — THY SOUL

THROUGH vaster spaces than thy thought-wings compass. Through the long eternities of never ceasing motion, I — thy soul, must wander, waiting, ever waiting for the hour to strike when thou, the body linked to me through all the vanished ages, may clear-eyed look into my face and know me as I am, for now, alas, thou art a living lie; the light of truth is far away from thee, and thou hast taken of my strength to build that lie.

"The Path" is hard to tread for thee, for thou hast made it hard. Thinkest thou that selfsame path is easier for me? I needs must walk therein until thine eyes are opened, and thou seest through the veil of flesh which thou hast built and closely folded round about thee, lest thou be compelled against thy will to see the naked truth; for well thou knowest thou must shrink abashed and terror-stricken, if its glorious light fall full upon thee now.

But one day surely that same light will pierce the veils despite thy frantic clutch upon them, and as thou bearest all its searching beams, so wilt thou bind me closer far to thee, or drive me forth unbound and desolate, compelled to leave thee to the Jinns[1] thou hast evoked.

---

[1] *Jinn* (*Arabic*, "to hide") — an elemental spirit. According to Arabic mythology, jinns were created from a pure smokeless flame and cannot be perceived by any of the five basic human senses. As with any elemental spirit, they can either invisibly assist or harm people. King Solomon was known to have power over jinns, thanks to a special stone in his possession. The jinns helped him build the Temple in Jerusalem.

I STAND AND WAIT

Look, my beloved, I stand at the gate and wait. Wait, while my knees bend low, my back bows down 'neath the weight of the heavy load I must bear, lest over-weariness come upon me, the gate swing shut, the latch fall into place, and thus shut out for aye some wayworn child who through my entreaties has entered the path that leads to the mount of transfiguration.

My outstretched hands must needs fend off the Guardian of the Threshold[1] lest he close the gate ere the threshold is cleared and leave but a part of thy mangled form on either side of the gate.

Then canst thou not bring me oil for my anointing, relief for my straining muscles and a kerchief to wipe the bloody sweat from my face? Bring them *thyself* from the farther land. I may not enter the nearer land to ease mine own self till thou hast passed the gate, for thou hast bound my body to the gate supports by the network of thy weakness.

I plead not for release, but that thou shouldst bring me the 'kerchief and oil — bring them *thyself*.

---

[1] *Guardian of the Threshold* or *Dweller on the Threshold* — the embodiment of one's internal negative essence that has been formed over the course of one's many lifetimes. One's spirit is set to meet with them before one's entrance into the Higher World. All one's weaknesses, vices, and shortcomings that were present in oneself on the Earth intensify manifold. They clothe themselves in visible, most attractive and seductive images to captivate and devour one's consciousness to such an extent that one no longer has either the strength or desire to cross the Threshold into the Supreme World, and so remains in the lower layers of space. Therefore, it is necessary that we prepare ourselves for the meeting with the Dwellers on the Threshold already during our stays in our physical bodies on the Earth, eliminating all shortcomings in ourselves. A trial by the Dwellers on the Threshold, produced by both their own and others' selves, also awaits everyone in the material world who has decided to follow the path of discipleship.

BE MERCIFUL TO GOD

Poor, weak and fickle, blind and feeble human soul, not even fully born, yet daring and defying God in ignorance of the effects of sacrilege so heedlessly committed.

The vaults of Heaven echo with the calls of the released who fain would draw me from thee, saying, "What is this man to thee that thou shouldst sacrifice thyself for him"? Yet all the treasures of the myriad spheres which jostle mine can never yield to me what I would lose in losing thee.

Man cries to God for pity in his horn' of trial, but never sees that God might even cry to man for pity in an horn when in his cowardice, his faithlessness and in ignorance man opens wide the door of Hell and leaps therein in his mad search for that he never yet has earned — the peace of all fulfillment — and so compels the Christ, the firstborn son of God, to enter Hell again, and yet again.

The loss of hand or foot will often send a man despairing to his tomb; yet man will tear apart the heart and limbs and body of his God, by tearing faith and love and mercy from his soul — the body of his God — and not perceive his cruelty until too late to stay his hand.

Be merciful to God, thou son of man, and God will mercy find for thee, in that dark hour when all alone thou standest forth to meet the Dweller on the Threshold of the future, and battle for thy right to live again as Man.

THE FACE OF CHRIST

Through all the long, long day, at morn and noon and night, we cry to Thee, Thou Christ of God. At morn we hail Thee King and build a throne and seat Thee there; by noon we tear Thee down, deny that we have ever known Thee, and, ere falls the night, with fulsome flattery or jest we plant the kiss of foul betrayal on Thy lips, and cowardly or stupidly stand by and see Thee nailed upon the cross. And Thou, each day that we in turn do crucify

Thee afresh, dost look into our eyes with tenderness, compassion, yet in sorrow past all telling; and nevermore while life and reason last, may we forget those eyes of Thine, those limpid pictures of the woes of all the world, nor fail to recognize that one wherein is limned the part that we have played in all that anguished woe.

Ah, human race, how great the price which day by day is paid again and yet again to raise each unit of the mass to heights where it may see the face of Christ in every human eye, and understand that only by a brother's need, a sister's pain, can one in justice gauge the help which should be given.

MY "LITTLE ONES"

GENTLE, tender, obedient, fit dwellers for the habitations of light — though now wandering in wild jungles where herd the human beasts of prey, or through the stony byways which thy brothers have prepared for thy weary feet, in ignorance of the law of final retribution — to thee and such as thee, would I speak a word of promise.

Though thine head be now bowed low; though thine heart pulsate with the thud of the fallen stone, though thy feet are torn and bleeding — yet shall the weight of thy brother's sin be lifted from thy neck, the blood once more course through thy veins with the bounding life of the days of thy youth; and I, even I, will cast aside the stones from thy path and deliver thee from the power of the human beasts of prey. Thou shalt be led to altars set on high, where thou mayest give thanks for the glory shed upon thy life; and power shall be given thee to reach down thy hand and help thy fallen brother to thine own side on the mountaintop.

THE DELIVERER

WILL nothing, life or death, the loneliness of the wilderness, the screams of the mob, the heights or the depths, open the eyes of the skeptic to the truth?

From the first gleam of light thrown on the law of gravitation; from the first observation of the moon's influence on the tides, life and law have been pouring out streams of corroborative evidence to every open mind, to the fact that "like seeks like," and seeks that it may kill, and kills that it may raise to higher fields of action, that which it kills. In terror, in despair, or for the sake of self-indulgence, man casts away the only prop that can possibly hold him safely to the Path — his faith in God — the ultimate Good, and refuses to see that only by the pain he suffers, the sacrifice he is compelled to make (whether he will or nay), his sorrow, repentance and final surrender, can he grow toward God and can gain full Illumination.

Like as every grain of sand, leaf of tree, sense or organ of body has developed by stress and strain, and all that action of life which impels to stress and strain and consequent suffering, so it is that all the best in man can only grow by suffering; and yet the slightest pain, the least sacrifice, the faintest trace of coming sorrow will arouse the demons in his nature to activity, and they will force him to yield them all of their desires (however hard the blows he strikes at their behest must fall upon some other suffering soul); until the hour of his deliverance has come.

If all the power he arouses at the call of those demoniacal forces might be turned in the right direction, the pain would vanish, the sacrifice become joy past telling, the desire for self-indulgence change to spiritual satisfaction, but Fear, the paralyzer, seizes him in its grip and only requires a breath of suspicion to cause him to relinquish his power and all that he has hitherto believed in or hoped for. Make way for the Deliverer. Enthrone the power of Endurance.

THE HEART OF A WORLD

TREAD softly, my child; breathe lightly, mine own. The sacred place of a breaking heart hath power to bow down the heads of Angels, to hush the wild shrieks of the Demons, and hold e'en the Hammer of Thor[1] suspended in space when the last fretted strand is parting.

Be still, little ones, you are standing today on most holy ground, for the Mother-heart of a world is breaking, and with it thy Father's heart.

The Devas[2] are raising the altar, and gathering the incense, grain by grain, as 'tis wrung from the sweat of despairing Souls; and the stars are clearing a path through the heavens that the Holy Fire may descend and kindle the Living Sacrifice of broken and contrite hearts. In the smoke of its burning the "seeing" eye may descry a vision of Law fulfilled and of Love, redeemed from bondage to sense, enthroned forevermore.

Go softly, be silent my child. Behold, and listen!

THE WHEEL OF TIME

Restless, Unsatisfied, Faithless Children:
Know ye that no power can stop the Wheel of Time to which I as well as thou art bound securely by fetters of our own forging? The more thou strainest at the fetters, the more they will cut into thy quivering nerves and flesh. By twisting thy tortured form to catch a glimpse of some other way which thou thinkest may haply be on the other side of the Wheel, thou dost only succeed in crushing thy head between the spokes.

Will ye leave me again as ye have so oft before, to bear the burden of your woe alone, while you go back to the slimy depths of the underworld amid the creeping things that weave their webs of Lust, Avarice and Selfishness about you — till ye are helpless

---

[1] *Thor* (*Old Norse*, "thunder") — the god of thunder in Scandinavian mythology; the son of Odin and Freya, and the chief of all elemental spirits. The word *Thursday* takes its name from Thor. *Thor's hammer* was a weapon that had the form of the *swastika*: the most archaic as well as the most sacred and universally respected solar symbol.

[2] *Deva* (*Sanskrit*, "shining one") — a god, deity, or celestial being, whether good, bad, or indifferent. Devas inhabit the "three worlds," which are the three planes above us. In Hinduism, there are 33 groups or 330 million of them.

in their meshes, and bound more hopelessly than ever upon that Wheel from which ye seek release?

O that my words were arrows that they might pierce your hardened hearts — that my thoughts were flames of love that they might kindle the dead embers on the cold altars of your souls!

SPIRITUAL BIRTH

LET not weariness of flesh or travail of Soul plunge you into sloughs of despair or discouragement. Ye cannot yet behold the dawn of new life — the fruition of your long travail.

Know ye not that the spiritual man cometh to birth in the silence, coldness and darkness of the Soul's midwinter, as doth the new life of the tree which seemeth cold and dead, whilst within the shelter of trunk and branch a new life-stream is rising, which shall bring forth healing and beauty when the long winter be passed? Think ye the future foliage, flower and fruit hath knowledge of the newly risen life-stream which is to bring them forth from the unseen, the unmanifest?

It is ever he who is willing to lose his life that shall find it. The pure life-stream which sprang forth from Infinity may be dammed up by willful evil, and made a receptacle for vile refuse, the flotsam and jetsam of human infirmities, and can only be clarified by pain, anguish and toil.

Tear down thine own peculiar dam, whate'er it cost thee, that the stream — purified by thy toil and suffering — may again flow back to its source, bearing on its bosom thy cargo of experience, and receiving in return the impulse to new life, new birth.

THOU WANDERER

COME back to me, my child! Thou wanderer — come, ere falls the night of life, and all enwrapped with shadows dense thou canst not see the way.

As deep hath called to deep across the centuries of time, so have I called to thee, and in thine egotistic blindness every path save one — the right one — draweth thee afar from me, and I must fain stand still and see thee go to certain sorrow.

The star which draws thee now is not the home thou seekest, nor canst thou reach the nearer star where I now stand, unless thou now wilt take my hand and let me lead thee home.

I do not threat thee, child of mine, but with my soul in arms against thy foes, I plead with thee to turn thy back on all the voices of the night, and though it be on sharpened rocks which pierce thy feet, retrace thy steps — come back to me.

THE HOMAGE OF THE HEART

THINK not to gird the laurel leaves of earthly fame upon the brow of him whom countless hosts of Light hail, "Victor!" in Life's lists. What careth he for tilings — for sense illusions? Purified by fire, bereft of pride, what king of earth or angel of the skies hath power to lead him to the throne where Maha Deva[1] awaiteth his appearance?

Alone, unheralded, he came upon the screen of time; alone he lived and died; alone he must ascend the steps — the spheres strewn with the vanquished and the slain of long past ages.

Each hard fought vantage ground he wins gives footing to another who hard beset doth follow; each plunge into the stream which flows from Maha Deva's head doth shower with cleansing drops some other weary soul too weak to reach their source.

The homage of thine heart alone will strengthen him for future battles with the hostile dwellers on "The Path" who fain would stop his way. Love imparteth strength for stern endurance and he may not lay down his arms and crown himself until you too stand by his side, a conqueror in truth.

---

[1] *Maha Deva (Sanskrit)* — the Great God.

TO THE NEOPHYTE[1]

To attain the goal of perfection — that goal where the consciousness of mortal man identifies itself with all the purity, power and glory of the divine, the inner Self — the candidate must pass through the Fires of Renunciation which alone can yield the Waters of Regeneration wherewith the sin-stained sheathes of Soul are purified. While passing through the fires or struggling in the waters, Victory will seem unattainable.

A silence, vast, deep, incomprehensible, comes over the neophyte when the supreme test of patient endurance of pain and suffering is at an end; his arms clasp but empty air as he raises them beseechingly to the Great Self for succor, for strength to bear the unutterable loneliness that envelops and falls like a pall about him. But it will pass, aye, pass it must, and in the peace that succeeds each hard won fight, there conies a sense of knowledge and power unspeakable — the guerdon of the travailing soul.

The indescribable sadness which invariably follows each successful battle with the lower self is natural; for as the candidate mounts each rung of the ladder of sentient life, he must grope around in the darkness for the next rung upon which to place his weary feet, until the eye of the soul is able to see — beyond the darkness — the star that shines overhead, the Star of Initiation.[2]

---

[1] *Neophyte* (*Greek*, "newly planted") — a beginner; also designates the disciples of lower degrees of the Great White Lodge.
[2] *Initiation* — the practice of initiation or admission into the sacred Mysteries, taught by the Hierophants and learned priests of the Temples, is one of the most ancient customs. This was practiced in every old national religion. In Europe, it was abolished with the fall of the last pagan temple. In the days of old, the Mysteries, according to the greatest Greek and Roman philosophers, were the most sacred of all solemnities as well as the most beneficent, and greatly promoted virtue. The Mysteries represented the passage from mortal life into finite death and the experiences of the disembodied Spirit and Soul in the world of subjectivity.

THY STAR AND MINE

WHEREFORE pourest thou forth streams of wrath upon thy brother's head — when amidst the flashing gems that deck the Mantle of the Gods, he finds a single one more beautiful to his simple vision than all the starry host that thou dost worship?

But for a difference in degree, the same light shineth through each and all — the same hand guideth all. The brilliant galaxy might well blind a too sensitive eye, when the mild beams of a single star in an azure field, would fall with tender blessings into depths where soul sight yet was holden. Rejoice with him that he hath seen even the first glimmer of light, and whisper to thine own heart: "Be still."

The King hath many crowns, each of different hue and guise. The one he gives to me would ill become my Lord — the Warrior of the Skies.

RENUNCIATION

IT IS NOT by renouncing the thing of lesser value nor those pleasures whose edges have become dulled to the cloyed senses, that the narrow path to the Gods is made plain. That path lies hidden within thine heart and many tendrils of intense desire must ruthlessly be torn apart ere its golden portals be disclosed.

Do not think that any unselfish effort for others is ever lost or wasted. As the rose attracts, holds, and then gives forth its life in terms of fragrance and beauty, so does the aroma of every true, unselfish act ascend as sweet incense to the footstool of the Gods — to return with added power as blessings for humanity.

"He that loseth his life shall find it," for it is only by renunciation, only by waiting in the darkness when there is no light, until the Way opens and the shadows disappear, bearing the pain, loving the causer of the pain, that the light from the great Father-love can break through the Christ to thee, thou child of Christ.

On the first mount thou shalt find a Cross; on the second mount, thy Transfiguration.

THE BIRTH OF THE SOUL

WHEN Eros,[1] the Star of Love, flashes a gleam of light into the hidden chamber of the heart, it stirs to life and action the sleeping Soul therein. With tender touches Love plumes the pinions of the Soul for flight to some other point in space where yet another Soul, lost in slumber, awaits its coming — for Love alone can bring the Soul to birth.

Ye daily clasp the hand and gaze into the eyes of soulless beings. But too often the riven casket alone remains to mark the spot where once dwelt the Splendor of God — driven thence by lack of sustenance: for the Soul hath need of daily food no less than hath the body. That which imparts life, sustains life — and Love is Life.

THE FRUIT OF THE TREE

THE Wisdom apples of the Tree of Life hang high on the topmost boughs, and only he who has won the power of far-reaching and strength for high climbing; only he who can keep his head cool and clear and his feet from slipping, can pluck and eat of that fruit.

It is the daily food of the Gods and only the Godlike man, armed with a purified will, can prevail over the Dragon that eternally guards the roots of that tree.

On its lower branches hang the silver apples of Knowledge, and he who hungers for that fruit must pluck it with the hand of Experience, gained through ceaseless search for hidden causes in the hearts of people and tilings.

He must find and destroy the worm of self coiled in the core of the apple he has plucked, and win the soul power of discrimination for by that alone can he find the Seed — the matrix wherein is accomplished the birth of Hermes,[2] or Wisdom.

---

[1] *Eros* (*Greek*, "love") — the God of Love in Greek mythology.
[2] *Hermes* — a Greek name for Thoth, the Egyptian God of Wisdom.

CHILDREN OF LIGHT

FREEBORN children of Light, what have ye to do with darkness? Darkness, the distorted offspring of Hate and Pride; darkness, the illusive ensnarer, the betrayer of mind, the glamor which blinds and leads into hopeless captivity the struggling soul; then leaves it to beat its tender wings against gross form until exhausted it sinks into apathy or despair.

Ye are Gods! Death hath no power over ye, conditions cannot bind ye; ye are Masters of Destiny if ye so will. Rulers over divine kingdoms. No God, no devil can banish ye from it or wrench it from ye — but alas, ye may renounce it by refusing to rule in righteousness and peace.

Ye are beyond the law for ye are Spirit, and Spirit is liberty, but mark ye, Liberty is not License, it is self-surrender, selflessness, unity, while License begets separateness, the great heresy.

Lay not thine head in the dust of the earth, for so the armies of the Shadow shall trample ye underfoot. Go forward with faith and lo, the serried ranks of the Hosts of Light shall encompass ye, and together ye shall win in the battle of the ages.

The Christ shall lead thee, He who holdeth the hearts of men in his keeping and will not let them go, thine own true self, the Warrior of Light.

THE EARTHBORN GOD

REASON'S votaries — blind leaders of the blind — shepherdless sheep, straying in barren, waterless wastes, in treacherous quagmires; making dwelling places at the foot of fiery mountains, at the mercy of the Demons who are but sleeping, or in the beds of old rivers, the waters of which shall once more return and overflow their banks — know each of you, that the wild beasts of the forests, the lizards sunning themselves on thy thresholds, interpret the signs of the times far better than thou — thou who hast enthroned earthly reason, and cast down the God of ancient

Wisdom — thou who hast set on high the darkness of the lower mind and quenched the Light of Intuition!

The wild beast fleeth from the path of the storm; thou seekest that path upon which to build thy resting place; nor canst thou flee if thou wouldst, for thou hast weighted thy feet with the lead of possessions, and art caught — as it were — in a net of things.

What boots it to thee that a warning voice from the mountaintop rings out again and again; thou canst hear but the clink of gold in the marketplace and the beguiling voice of thine earthborn God — human reason.

THE WINE OF LIFE

LISTEN, My Beloved:
Pour not with lavish hand upon the earth the wine of life — that sparkling draught thy mother Maia[1] gave thee at birth for strength and succor 'gainst thine hour of need.

The dregs that remain within the cup art but vile refuse, unfit to feed gross swine upon, though still mayhap retaining some faint flavor of the wasted wine. And if too vile too feed to swine — how canst thou offer such a gift to God, or lay it on Life's stone of sacrifice?

To the pure heart, all things in heaven and earth are pure; and if thine heart be pure, the cup of wine will overflow and turn to streams of light while still within thy grasp, carrying life and healing on their waves far down the distant centuries of time.

THE GUERDON OF HUMILITY

HEARKEN unto me, thou who standest with straightened neck in the path of the coming Tempest, the powers of which are seeking to equilibrate the varied forms of life-forces thou hast called into action.

---

[1] *Maia (Greek)* — one of the seven daughters of Atlas and Pleione in Greek mythology, after whom the seven stars of the Pleiades were named; the mother of Hermes.

Bend low thine head, lest the Demons, the Satellites of the Storm-King strike at thine eyes and destroy thy clear vision — and thou canst not find the path which leadeth to safety.

Pride ever precedeth destruction. Only when thou hast gained the guerdon of true humility canst thou stand erect in safety, for then only hast thou power to don the Armor of sure protection — the Armor of Compassion.

THE LOVE DIVINE

Can the Rose tree burst into bloom if turned downward in the earth?

Can the Coral Polyp attach its reef to the clouds of the air?

Can Water freeze in the path of the Electric bolt?

No more can man live without love.

No more can man attain his full spiritual growth away from the rays of the Sun of Righteousness, the warmth of Infinite Love, than he can attain to physical perfection if shut away from light and air.

From that love emanated the first impulse of his being; in it must eventually be absorbed the last. He may exist for a time in ignorance of that love, but he will not realize what life means — for to such, only a cold negative existence is at most possible on earth, and a hopeless looking forward to final annihilation: for without Love there is no life either here or hereafter.

THE BIRD OF LIFE

Thinkest thou, child of my soul, to climb the steep path to thy Father's home with thy feet weighted with the viscid mud of the underworld? Thinkest thou to reach thy Father's heart by means of the power thou hast filched from thy weaker brother — or that thou canst reach Love's heights through Hatred's depths? Build thou a nesting place in thy brother's love, and the overshadowing wings of the Bird of Life will cover both thee and him. If thou buildest elsewhere, the fierce talons of the Bird will tear asunder and scatter the fragments of that nest to the four winds of heaven; then shalt thou be left homeless and comfortless, and thy brother sad and lonely, for thou hast robbed him of that which is his by right of the divine brotherhood which dwelleth within his heart as well as within thine own.

THE ARMOR OF FAITH

IF THY nearest and dearest friend stand in its path, the same snake that strikes its poisonous fangs into thy tender flesh, will strike at thy friend with redoubled power gained through the life blood thou hast unwittingly yielded up.

Protect thy friend, as well as thyself, by clothing thyself with the impenetrable armor of implicit faith.

A single snowflake, carelessly rolled amidst others of its kind, exposed to rain, and left to the power of the Ice King for a time, will make a missile with which thou mayest fell a giant.

A careless gesture, a thoughtless word rolled amidst others of like character, exposed to the withering blasts of a foul mind, may strike down and cripple the soul thou lovest best.

LOVE'S CONQUEST

PEACE and Power come swiftly to the man who lifteth his sister from the depths of her despair, to plant her feet on the first step of the ladder of Renunciation. The Law of Compensation will one day set his feet on the highest step of that same ladder — the step that leadeth to the door of the Inner Sanctuary.

Woe and Retribution fall swiftly upon the head of that woman, who, to enhance her own value in the eyes of the one her eyes are fixed upon, wantonly destroys his trust in the honor of another. The murdered trust will arise from its tomb in mighty power to avenge the wrong.

With joy and gladness shining as the gems of a coronet upon their placid brows; with feet shod with the sandals of full reparation — upward, always upward, passeth the two made one, who have vanquished their deadliest foe, and raised from its ashes the Peace of Purity — who have built in their hearts a nesting place for the Bird of Love, and opened their ears to the mystery and splendor of the Song of Life — that joyous song, the first sweet notes of which break down forever the wall of separation between two souls, uniting them in the single stream that floweth ever onward to the Ocean of Infinity.

THE PATH OF DUTY

WOULDST thou turn thy face away from thine earthly love at the bidding of another? If so, thou art not worthy of that love.

How much less worthy then art thou of spiritual love, if so be thou fleest from the path of duty at the behest of another who hath not even won the power to discern the path wherein he himself might most perfectly unfold. How much less power, then, hath he to guide thee aright.

LIFE'S OPPORTUNITIES

LIFE'S opportunities, like angel visitants, pass swiftly, silently — and if we fail to catch the first faint echo of their coming footfalls, or, all untrained to action swift, we fail to seize and force them to reveal their hidden power, their passing is for aye.

They are the spans by which our lives are measured — a ladder straight and long — with one step leading into Heaven, and yet another reaching down to Hell — the mile stones 'twixt our puny littleness and the measureless largeness of God.

THE HARP OF INFINITY

FORGET not, child of my heart, that thou art a builder of worlds: that millions uncreate await but the touch of thy fingers on the strings of the Harp of Infinity to spring into being as

Paeans of Victory and Life, or discords Satanic, which needs must end in evil and death.

Strike full clear tones, that thy place may be opened in the Choir of Heaven.

AS YE SOW

HE WHO dips his pen in the bitterness of gall and wormwood and therewith destroys the peace of his brothers, by the same act opens the latent centers of poison in his own aura, bringing upon himself disease and spiritual degeneracy. The pen will turn to a sword which, though it pass through his brother's heart, will lie embedded in his own at last.

THE SOUL OF SONG

WOULDST thou, Musician, sing the Song of Life, in tones that gods and men may hear and, hearing, thrill with rapture? Then thou must, by long and patient plodding, strive to reach the innermost recess of every congery of force — of every thing and being, and reaching it, to make thyself a part of it.

Thou canst not sing a tone of it aright if separated from the Soul which is its life; for, rising, falling, swelling with an agony of bliss, the tone called forth from hidden places, responds in fullness only to a soul more hungry than itself; and called by such an one it rushes forth and intermingling with that other Soul it rises in a glorious burst of sound too fine, too strong, for mortal ears to hear and bear.

THE GOAL

AS POINTETH the mariner's needle to the white Star of the North, however the waves of the ocean swell or the winds of heaven roar, so must thou point thy will to the Star of thine ambition. Instability and change may be thy brother's pleasure, but they should find no place in one whose feet are strongly set upon the Path of God. Ah, take thou thought, set thine ambition high. Love and Peace will be worth infinitely more to thee than myriads of lesser prizes, however brightly their reflected light may glow before thine earthly eyes.

MYSTERY OF MYSTERIES

POOR, desperate, self-tortured Human Heart; large with the largeness of God, narrow as the path of eternal life! Selfishly grasping the straws of life for thine own glory, carelessly sacrificing thy Royal inheritance, unwitting that such sacrifice is the crown of thy life-series of mistakes.

Blind, yet having the power of infinite perception; dumb, yet possessing the sweetness of Angel tongues or the virulence of Demon speech.

Mystery of Mysteries art thou; truly, thy name is Legion, thy nature Incomprehensible.

WING THY HEART HOME

WING thy Heart home, thou wanderer in desert places. Though needles of sharp cacti pierce thy feet, and scorching sands fill thine eyes; though not a living thing speak thee guidance, yet shalt thou find the path and keep it to the journey's end. For where the heart hath found surcease, there must perforce the weary body follow. So, once again, I say, wing thy heart home, mine own.

THE CHILD OF LOVE

WHEN your gratitude to me becomes a subject for reasoning — when you can convince yourself that you have earned or deserve that which has been given you in love — then have you thrown down the Angel of Selflessness and set up an Idol to Self.

As gushes forth the spring of water over the thirsty soil, heedless of where its drops may fall, delighting, reveling, in its power to give, even to the uttermost, so gushes from the heart of the child of love, pure gratitude.

GOD'S THOUGHT

AH, LITTLE one, God's latest thought. Ah, soul reborn on earth from infinite domains, dost think thou earnest hence thyself; hence to a world of woe? God *thought* thee into being; winged thy soul with love and sent thee on the way to find those other thoughts of His — thy brother men, and intermingling with them, form a pool wherein the Light which lightens all the world may be reflected.

LOVE'S ABODE

MY LITTLE ones, sit ye here with me in the twilight, while peace falls as a curtain over the turmoil of the day. Let the softly whispered "Hush!" of earth and sky fall on your inner ears as your heads are bent for the benison of the brooding Spirit of Rest. I, too, would speak to thee, weary footsore traveler o'er stony places and desert sands.

I have seen thine uplifted hands, have heard the low cry which passed unheeded by those most near, most dear, to you, and would say again and yet again — seek not surcease from pain and longing in the haunts of men, the hearts of women, for it is not there.

Dig deep through the encrusted layers of your own souls till you find the spot which Love hath chosen for its dwelling place — the nesting place of the Infinite. Ah, well I know the tale is trite and old. Too oft hath it fallen on unheeding ears. But it is ever new to some sad soul, and when you have found that spot, it will be all things to you, for it holds the Key to the beginning and end of thy travail — to the unspeakable heights and depths of the manifest

Universe — the glory of the Shekhinah[1] — the crown of thine own and all other lives.

THE TAIL OF THE DRAGON

THE tail of the Dragon is coiled about the Star of Destiny. Down, down through the fields of space — through the ranks of the Rishis[2] is that Star now drawn.

Howl, ye sons of Men, ye Daughters of Earth! War, Panic, Desolation cometh upon you. In the marketplaces will ye cry, "Nine loaves of bread for a penny," and there will be none to take.

Ye call upon the Lord with your lips and defile His image with your hands! Ye dash clown the cup of Life from the lips of your brethren, and will not drink thereof yourselves! Ye call out "Liar, Thief, Adulterer!" while ye are bars, thieves, adulterers. Ye are thieves, for ye steal the fair fame of your brethren; ye are adulterers, for ye cohabit in lust of mind and eye, and bring forth spawn of Hell for your brethren's corruption.

Ye seek a sign and are blind to the signs ye have received.

Liars and hypocrites, who sit in high places, the Dragon will bring you low. Your measure is all but full, and Mercy draweth close the veil over her face till your times are fulfilled.

ROUSE YE!

POOR, petty figment of matter enmeshed in mud of thine own making! Ye would draw down the stars to minister to your puling cries! Ye ask, but will raise no hand to receive the offered gift! Ye listen, and hear naught but the echo of your piping voices. Cowards! Renegades from the battle of life — unworthy the great sacrifice offered you! Ye turn and rim from a kitten's claws into the mouth of a hungry wolf! Unstable as water, fickle as wind, neither

---

[1] *Shekhinah* (*Hebrew*, "dwelling") — the presence of God; the veil of the Absolute.
[2] *Rishi* (*Sanskrit*, "sage") — a Hindu sage or saint; an Adept; the inspired one.

Heaven nor Earth hath room for you — while in truth, ye lay back on your earthy oars in pitiable self-sufficiency and cry "Ho, Comrade! Behold how great a man I am!"

Rouse ye! Mount as have mounted the suns now circling in motion swifter than thought in yonder vaults! Shine as doth shine those flaming thoughts of God that people the aisles of Heaven; for ye are of God, and all power is yours if ye seek aright!

WHICH OF THE THREE?

Ho, soldiers of the Grand Army of the Great White Lodge![1] Know ye not, the War of the Ages is on? The warriors are lining up for battle. Where do ye belong? Are ye warriors of Light or of Darkness?

Are ye banner men of true and loyal heart, or are ye cowards, traitors? Can ye grasp and hold the colors, the words of truth brought to you under fire, bind them on the hilts of your swords, emblazon them on the banners ye bear, and stand forth to battle for them with the natural foe of your common humanity?

Go, with the Rallying Cry of the Red Ray[2] on your lips, the light of high purpose flashing from your eyes, ready to do or to

---

[1] *Great White Lodge* or *Great White Brotherhood* — the Hierarchy of Light existing on the Earth. The word *White* here symbolizes spiritual purity and has absolutely no association with ethnicity or skin color. It indicates the White Light that, upon splitting, yields the seven colors of the rainbow, each of which symbolizes one of the Great Masters, and vice versa — the seven colors of the rainbow that result in the White Light after fusion. In the White Brotherhood, there is no distinction of race, gender, color, nationality, culture, creed, or religion.

[2] *Rallying Cry of the Red Ray* — an invocation to the Creative Forces of the Universe, published in 1900:

Enter in, dear Father, enter in, dear Mother,
Enter in, dear sister, enter in, dear brother,
Enter in, dear Father, enter in, dear Mother,
And another little sister and another brother too.
Enter in, dear Father, enter in, dear Mother,
And the sons and daughters of the Lord Our God.

die, as seemeth best, upon that field above which soars the gage of battle — the Soul of man!

Or will ye steal from the ranks while the war cry is sounding, kill the bearer of the Orders, seize and hide the message in your own selfish hearts until ye find a safe retreat wherein, secure from other eyes, ye may gloat over it as misers o'er their gold, under the delusion that ye are saving your souls alive?

Will ye join in the din and strife of the battle, raise your voices to stifle the moans of your comrades, recklessly trample the wounded 'neath your feet, pile up the bodies of the slain to cover your retreat to the enemy's ranks, all unknowing the fate that is closely following your steps?

The grains of corn now in process of grinding by Nemesis,[1] flow fine as mist into the bins the avenger has built and the blood of the slain in battle will yield power for the milling.

To which of the three divisions dost thou belong? I ask thee. Thee — each in turn, enlisted soldiers of the Army of the Great White Lodge, thou must answer the question. Thine own soul makes demand and will not be denied.

LOVE THE AVENGER

GODS may thunder, Angels may whisper, "thou shall not," "I pray thee not" to awakened passion in the human heart, yet the glamor cast by elemental fiends[2] over the mind of men and women, first narcotizes, then drives them on, on to satisfaction and satiation, and finally into hells of their own making, such as devils might envy them the power to make.

For God — Love — is a jealous God. In so far as God is jealous, he is jealous for Love's sake, for Love is higher than any God

---

[1] *Nemesis* (*Greek*, "to give what is due") — the goddess of retribution and vengeance in Greek mythology.
[2] *Elementals* — the spirits of the elements of Earth, Water, Air, and Fire (for example, jinns, elves, undines, dwarfs, salamanders, sylvans, etc.). These are blind and irresponsible forces of Nature, subject to the control of the will. They can be used to produce various phenomena.

conceived by mortal mind: and Love betrayed by passion surely bringeth vengeance upon the betrayer — vengeance that will eat the heart, as worms may eat the vitals of the dead. Passion gratified at the expense of Love — illicit love — will turn to gall within the human breast and embitter life, at every turn, and worst of all, it will destroy the very marrow in the bones of the soul. It will leave a man or woman without a vestige of self-respect, and in place of the self-respecting man there will arise a prating effigy, a simulacrum, a thing without a soul.

Stretch out your trembling fingers, ye passion-tossed of the world.

Twang the strings of that harp of the soul, until it has lost the pure tone that the Angels of the Throne attuned it by, if ye will, and then quiver in agony at the harsh discords your fingers will thereafter draw from that dishonored harp.

You must play upon it whether you will or nay, and the keynote by which its strings might be attuned is beyond your reach, if Love has been abased, and vengeance has fallen.

LOOK DEEP

Child of Earth, look deep! The scum of a pool always rises to the surface. Be not deceived by that which lieth close at hand, but search the silent, waveless depths beneath, wherein lies thy peace.

GOD STILL LIVES

Arouse thee, thou who sittest in the darkness! Bestir thyself and weep, if smiles are no more possible. Better far that thou shouldst moisten thy parched soul with tears, than brood o'er vanished joys in silence and despair. The future yet remains untried — and God still lives.

Inaction breeds despair, which, like all other lifeless things, must quickly be entombed, ere like a poisonous plant it shall destroy all life within its sphere.

THE LIGHT OF PEACE

HE WHO prepareth a place for me, to him will I come in peace. Light from on high shall shed its radiance o'er his dwelling place, and he shall lie down in sheltered places. Darkness shall flee away, as fleeth the conscience-smitten from the law, and the glory of righteousness shall deck his form as with a garment sewn with precious gems.

COME FORTH!

COME forth from your hiding places, ye whom Lucifer hath frighted! Know ye not that darkness and the light of day can never dwell together in one place? And ye did seek the darkness, and the peace of nonfulfillment when the demon Fear assailed and sandaled you with coward's gear.

Light is fire, and fire will burn; but better far for thee the burn, the pain, the longing, than darkness and the ease it brings; which, while it soothes to sleep, will steal thy crown of life and hide it where thou canst not seek, then softly laugh, when thou, with outstretched arms, art wandering midst the outer spheres, a formless, shadowy thing, bereft of name, of home, of all but semi-consciousness.

A NEW CYCLE

THE eventide of a cycle has passed and the rays of the morning sun of a new cycle are tinging the horizon of your lives. Whate'er of shadow still remains in memory's vaults, will help to soften the aftermath of the high noon days to come, and serve as a screen on which to limn the outlines of a higher ideal than those you have pictured in former days, if so be you have gained the Spiritual Will that can wield the brush of pure Desire aright. But, Beloved, bear well in mind the note of warning I now sound — never dip *that* brush in the heart's blood of another human being. That blood would darken and spread o'er the form you limned till naught but a dull, red smear would remain to mark its place.

With brave, strong hand, dip the holy brush into the infinite depths of Love's sacrifice of Self, draw the lines straight and true by the rules of the Higher Self, and an Ideal will flash forth upon that screen of the Soul, too strong, too beautiful, mayhap, for other eyes than thine to bear, yet pregnant with a radiant stream of life that, being born, will reach and feed all starving hearts within your sphere of touch.

THE ANGEL OF HEALING

WOULDST thou court the Angel of Healing for thy suffering friend? Then bring not gifts of sorrow's choosing, such as doth already sore afflict thy friend; for so, the Angel first must heal thine own infirmity ere passing to thy friend, for in the bringing, thou hast bound the gifts so close about thy form, they can no more be separate from thee until the healing Angel's touch hath struck thy fetters down and set thee free.

MAN

WALKING shadows of things that might have been; potential forms of things that are to be — God and man in one. Paradox supreme art thou, amidst a universe of paradoxes. Creatures of an hour, fast digging graves with your own hands your forms must fill. Angels of eternity fast building thrones your souls will grace. Who can measure your heights or sound your depths, thou mystery of mysteries?

VEILS OF THE SOUL

CHILDREN mine, with minds so like as yet the gaseous state of this Dark Star,[1] when, countless eons gone, the vapory, shifting masses separated, and to all-seeing eyes disclosed a dazzling tongue of flame, a softly shimmering light with here and there a peak or pinnacle of glowing fire, which hid a power unspeakable. Eons hence, a nearer balance will be struck between you and the world in which you live. The seeming vapory shadows veiling soul from soul, are in reality but background for the light concealed, a background upon which the vagaries, the dreams of man may fall. But the shades will lift and pass away forever when Light and Soul become again the One, as in the far away beginning.

LIFT UP YOUR HEADS

CAN ye see the faint flush of the daybreak, ye Children of Light? It hangeth low in the cosmic darkness as yet, but eyes not holden may catch a gleam of its brightness, ears not dulled hear the clarion note in the distance. The Day Star is rising, rising, rising, and, though sky and earth seem drenched with blood-red reflections — the first emanations of darkness — the golden light cometh to redeem, to sanctify, to bless the hard-pressed children of Maya.[2]

Lift up your heads, strengthen your weakened knees, bind closer the burdens ye bear, turn your eyes to the East, and watch, wait and work.

---

[1] *Dark Star* — the name given by the Masters to the Earth, which can become a bright star, being the "cradle of Gods." The true name of the Earth is *Tiamat*.
[2] *Maya* (*Sanskrit*, "illusion") — the illusive and transient nature of earthly reality and existence.

COME BACK

Come back to me, my children, wandering now in trackless wastes, without guide or compass save thy pride, thy self-sufficiency. Not e'en the sun in heaven can cut its deep wide swath alone, but needs must hold its place by power of other brighter suns. And thou, poor foolish one, because thou canst not always see a golden gleam of light upon the path I laid 'twixt thee and me, must darken more that path, that life, by all the pain and anguish thou canst lay upon it; and then, alas, cry out, there is no path, no light, no loving Father's hand to guide, to hold, to cheer amid the shadowy way of life, both you and I must tread, together or alone.

PRIDE

Far better were it for thee, would-be Child of the Stars, wert thou covered with the filth of sensuality, or the foul corruption of the marketplaces, than that thou shouldst stand upon the heights of worldly power, and loudly cry unto thy brethren, "Behold my virtue, bow to my accomplishments, bend low thy back that I may tread dry-shod the slimy pool in which thou art engulfed."

The pride which strips thee of all likeness to the Blessed Ones, will drag thee lower far than lieth now the meanest of thy brethren.

ENTER THE PATH

Hearken thou to the resonant voice of the Silence of Life, the voice of the Warrior bold which calleth to thee from the Place of Peace, powerfully, pleadingly, bidding thee open thine ears, conquer thyself, make room in thine heart for the bloom of thy soul long budded, and wearying sore for the power of fruition — the power by which thou canst see my face, and grasp the sword I hold in my hand. The power of the self-born, the warrior bold, alone can open the close-shut door of the hidden garden of life, and shelter give to the sorely pressed of earth.

Enter the Path; though the way may be rough, the end will bring thee power and peace and joy past human telling.

THE HOLY FLAME

Sons of my soul, my tears, children of my torment, why will ye not hasten to lay the wood and coals of tire upon the Seven Horns of mine Altar, that I may descend and bring again the Holy Flame to kindle them.

'Till ye lay wood and coals of fire upon the Seven Horns of mine Altar of your own free will, I must stand and wait.

With all the loud voices of earth, sky and sea, I cry unto you, while ye but stand and gape at each other, and fill your ears, that ye may neither see nor hear when Kamsa[1] steals that which is mine own, and that which one day ye would give a kingdom to possess.

CROSS AND CROWN

Children mine, desperate hunted things, weak supine exhausted ones, tortured, tempted, stricken creatures, *hear me* while yet I can speak to you. Passion crazed, you go from seeming flower to flower, knowing not, caring not that you go from hell to hell, and are so going because you have not yet the courage, the strength, the will, to look the demons of those hells in the face, grasp their throats, and *force* them back into their strongholds.

One among a thousand, a man or woman can see his or her only chance lies in "throttling the great Beast." As long as you can suffer a single qualm from the poison your friend has placed in your cup of life, as long as your enemy can find a tender spot on

---

[1] *Kamsa (Sanskrit)* — a tyrant ruler in Hindu literature. He was the brother of Devaki and shut her up in a dungeon for fear of the fulfilment of a prophecy stating that a son of his sister should dethrone and kill him. Notwithstanding the strict watch kept, Devaki was overshadowed by Vishnu, the Holy Spirit, and thus gave birth to Krishna, the Savior of the Hindus. Like King Herod, Kamsa slew thousands of newborn babies while seeking Krishna among the shepherds and cowherds that concealed him.

your exposed parts in which to plant a dagger, you are helpless, unguarded.

As long as a word, a look, a blow or a caress, can start the blood madly bounding through your veins, you are naught but tender nestlings, bound to be devoured by man and beast.

Hear me. Strive to learn to *love pain*. Open your hearts to crucifixion, that you may so seek the Strength which is in truth your Real Life.

THE LIGHT OF LIFE

Sensation's offspring, child of Earth thou art, though wrapped in fold on fold of starry light. Thine outer vesture masks a spirit stronger far than that which holds it bound but holds it only through its lack of love and power of sacrifice sublime, the love and sacrifice which is thy life, thine all.

Regain the poise, the equilibrium which held thy soul in balance true with all that lives and breathes; and which thou parted with in ignorance of all that foul ambition's curse would bring to thee and thy beloved. Strike for the freedom which is thine by birthright pure, and be no longer held by filmy threads which stay thy steps and will not let thee go.

The light of Life is all about, within and over thee. Open wide the portal of thy soul and send that light, like blessed dew, upon thy brethren wandering now in parched and desert places. It will return to thee tenfold the brighter, bringing on its waves the joy of life's fulfillment. But if thou hidest it, and will not let it shine for others now in darkness, it will but focus all its power upon thy selfish heart, and only ashes will remain to tell the long sad tale.

A PROPHECY

Drawn by will of the Daityas[1] from the uttermost ends of Maya's realms, swiftly foregather the clouds in the Eastern sky, hiding the light of the sun from the holden eyes of men.

---
[1] *Daityas* (*Sanskrit*) — Giants, Titans, and exoterically demons.

"Ha! Ha!" laugh the Daityas, "no God, no servant of the Lhas[1] can free the earthborn from our power, for we have o'ershadowed the source of their life; now can we stand and watch, while the brown and yellow slaves of our will wreak vengeance on those who defy our power."

Cry aloud, ye sons of earth, for the crashing of arms, the curses of the frenzied, the shrieks of the murdered, now ascend to the fast-barred gates of Devachan,[2] and the Gods heed not, for the hour of judgment is not yet passed. But hold, the Purified comes to burst asunder the chains that bind, to tear from their fastenings the bars of those gates. Then must awaken the Gods who sleep, for the new day will dawn. With swift flight will they come to the desolated earth; with their breath will they drive back the Daityas to their dwelling-place. They will open the inner and outer heavens, and pour down food and drink. They will bind up the wounds of the smitten, and bring the Holy Fire for the Altars long defiled. Peace and contentment will dwell on the earth for a thousand rounds. Love will conquer hate; and again, as of old, will the Gods dwell with man.

HOLD, AND LISTEN

HO, YE who hunger and thirst for the enthroned "Truth"; and yet look backward longingly into the gulf ye leave, ere lifting foot to take an upward step: Ye hesitate, or dare not stir, lest ye should meet Truth's searching eye, and stand revealed unto yourselves.

Ho! Coward, server of the god of Time, fouled with thy satiated lusts, and dank with hell's fulfilled ambitions — hold, and listen!

---

[1] *Lha* (*Tibetan*, "spirit") — the Spirits of the Highest Spheres.
[2] *Devachan* (*Tibetan*, "blissful realm") — the place of rest between incarnations in the Subtle World, akin to Paradise, in which spirits feel celestial bliss and are immersed in dreams in which they experience, with particular vividness and superior to earthly reality, all the happiest days and moments in their latest life.

Ho! Ye weary and faint-hearted, clutching in thine hand the emptied shell of that which held thy faith; too tired now to seek, too weak to reach Desire, sinking 'neath the weight the world hath lain on such as you: Listen all, to one who knows full well the thirst, the hunger and the heat; to one who knows, and once has waded blindly through the sloughs of sin. Listen ye to one who climbed the cross of earth's incessant woe, and nailed his body there for fellow men to smite; who drank the cup *ye* are too tired to lift, e'en to its dregs; who merged desire for death into desire for life, and made the cross a key to song immortal; to one who learned that even cowardice and shame might leap the gulf between the Hero and the slave by consecrated strife, and bind the wreath of all fulfillment on his brow.

Strike out — all ye who hear and heed!

CHRIST OR JUDAS?

Is it Christ or Judas! Ye who hold the scales of earthly power? Have ye yet chosen him whom ye would serve?

Choose ye must! The time is close at hand. The breath of angels now is held against your choosing.

The field of battle stretches far away, but ye are near the ever-living gage — the gage of man's self-consciousness.

With hand outstretched, betrayal graven on his fact, stands he who ever at the break of day leaps forth to greet each coming soldier of the Christ, who wearied from his journey long and tedious, crazed with longing for a draught from Lethe's[1] streams, too often falls beneath the spell, and wrapped in glamor of satanic weaving, looks, and listens, falls — and dies.

Art thou of that vast number, son of mine? Or canst thou see the Holy Grail I hold before thine eyes, and seeing, gird thyself

---

[1] *Lethe* (*Greek*, "oblivion") — one of the five rivers of the Hades underworld. All those who drank from this river experienced complete forgetfulness. In Greek mythology, Lethe is also the personification of forgetfulness and oblivion.

and fall in line behind the King of Kings, to die a mortal's death, mayhap — but yet to live eternally with Christ?

Will Christ or Judas hold thy mantle in the coming strife?

Choose ye must — and *now*!

THE GOD OF PAIN

IF THOU dost choose to learn by pain alone, and turnest far thy face from me when with my gourd in hand I stoop to give thee drink from water sweet which trickles from the font where Knowledge and its sister Power in friendly rivalry do vie to give thee all thy soul demands — then must I leave thee to the woe which willful disobedience doth bring to human kind.

The power of choice is thine, since the dawn of Kalpas[1] past, the Arhats[2] came to earth to dwell with man — in man; and if thou heedest not the voice of those who speak thee fair, what is there left for them or me to do but wait until the God of Pain hath chastened thee.

THE KING COMETH

HEAR ye the thunders of the Triple Six? Know ye not the hour of fulfillment is near at hand?

Thrice hath Merodach[3] slain the vultures that tear at the heart of the Sun God, and again must he bend bow and spear ere his task be done, and the glory of the 666 be revealed unto man.

Swifter than flight of arrow cometh the Deliverer to break asunder the chains that bind, and free the captive Prince. Never

---

[1] *Kalpa* (*Sanskrit*, "formation," "creation") — a long period or cycle of evolution.

[2] *Arhat* (*Sanskrit*, "worthy," "one deserving divine honors") — one who has attained the highest level of enlightenment; the Great Teachers are commonly referred to as Arhats.

[3] *Merodach* (*Chaldean*) — the God of Babylon, the Bel of later times; the Great God of Wisdom, or "he who resurrects the dead." He is the son of Davkina, Goddess of the lower regions, or the earth, and of Hea, God of the Seas.

again shall the fire of love be quenched with the waters of affliction, the trust of tender woman to be betrayed. Never again shall the Father's pride in his well-beloved plunge him into outer darkness.

The King cometh, and who shall prevail against him?

THE HOLY ANGEL, LOVE

TO DISGUISE the miry sloughs of human passion, hatred, murder, treachery and deceit, man hath used the most sacred of all sacred words — Love; knowing naught of the Holy Angel which it designates; ignorantly fearing not its misused power, which yet is great enough to hold the stars in place and guide the myriad lives of earth to heavenly bliss and back again to earth.

The darksomeness of blackest night is no more dense than is the mind that fails to see in Love, the firstborn Son of God: clothed in the vesture of that power which manifests Devotion pure and undefiled; the power which tears the gyves and fetters from the limbs of all the human race, and sets it free from bondage to the Wheel of Time.

MAKE CLEAN THINE HEART

O LITTLE man! O, foolish man! Webbed in the illusive changing scenes about thee, or rooted in the lowest sphere of human fear and passion, thou dost elect by means of potent Will to there remain — content and useless. Back into the faces of the Gods, thou throwest life's great opportunities untried, and draweth close the veil of ignorance around thee.

Why trample underfoot the seven-stringed Lute through which compassion's low sweet tone may stir thy soul to loftier deeds and aims? Why breathe a film of foul corruption o'er the Lens through which alone the light of Truth may fall on thee? Hast thou not heard the lime grows not on a thorn tree, nor yet a fig on a thistle? Make clean thine Heart, that so the sun-kissed heights of Love may image there the Soul that long hath watched o'er thee — that patiently awaits thine hour of waking.

THY HERITAGE

THICKEST thou the strength thou usest is thine because of merit won, or is the guerdon of thy labor? Then put away the thought, it ringeth false; for only is it thine by reason of thy unity with all that lives. Yet must thou labor with all diligence from early morn 'till close of day, that thou mayst add to that great sum of all the labor done by Gods and men, by means of which thy heritage, thy greater strength, is won, and will remain for rightful use, 'till life's long day is ended.

THE DRAUGHT OF LETHE

LOW have you fallen, sons of my Son, who in his greatness cast away the offered gift of endless peace, to win the right to say, "I Am." For ye would spurn the gift so hardly won by Him, ere ye would suffer pain of body or of soul, and often clutch with greedy hands the cup which holds the draught of Lethe, brewed and offered you by aliens to that Sun of Light who brought self-consciousness to man.

THE PLACE OF PEACE

WHY trouble your hearts and waste your precious time by dwelling on the evil done by those who wish you harm? Know you not that you lie in hands which have the power to hold you safe, and naught can compass you to your eternal hurt, save by your will?

A gnat can minister to your discomfort only as you fix your mind upon it or the wound it leaves.

Find the "Place of Peace," and friends and enemies alike will be but added blessings, for both will speak to you of God — the one of Love, the other of Forgiveness.

THE PATH

GO! Go quickly, to the place prepared for thee, False Fiend of Selfish Lust — disguised in Pleasure's changeful robes. Wouldst even thou drag down the "little ones" of Christ, into the slimy ooze where thou dost dwell, abhorred of God and man, that thou mayst rob them of all power, all purpose and all strength, and render them fit devotees and ministers to thee?

Strike! Strike hard and fast — Renunciation, Pain, ye Angels of the Arch of Heaven! Let loose the Keys fast clasped by hand to breast — Compassion's Keys — to all the heights, to all the starry corridors where dwells our Lord, and where awaiteth He the advent of His chosen. There the work for which past anguish hath prepared them, is pointed out by Him. None other hath the power to mark the way, for none but Christ hath climbed Transfiguration's heights and bridged the gulf of Hades'[1] hate, to open wide "The Path."

TO THE DEAD IN LIFE

AGAIN and again falls the hammer of the Gods, and the throbbing tones of the Anvil ring true on ears that hear. Blow follows blow on "The Iron Wheel" hot with the blast of the outraged Law. Higher and yet higher rise the flying sparks, filling the heavens with fiery streams which descend as scourges of pestilence, famine and flame.

Pile up your dead, ye dead in life. Hide them from view, lest their mangled forms cry vengeance upon you; then stand on their shallow graves, if ye can, and cry: "Great are we earthborn sons of Desire; Giants of Power, of Finance and Fame. Hasten, ye slaves of our dominant wills, cover the archives, the records, which prove we be passion-bred bastards of lustful desire for lands and silver and gold!"

---

[1] *Hades* — the Greek god of the underworld, and the underworld itself; a hell.

The stench of your evil poisons the air, and only blue flames from the hidden fires can render it fit for the breathing of those who come on the wings of the morning light to offer to fallen man the grip of the Lion's Paw.

Go on! Go on to the end, for ye will not hear. In thirst for Power, ye have blinded your eyes and ye cannot perceive ye are objects of scorn — butts for the play and the laughter of fiendish Jinns, who blind and deceive, who set wary traps into which ye trip, who gleefully laugh at the steel-ribbed vaults ye have crossed and recrossed with the currents of doom.

Again and again has the message gone forth; again and again doth the Master cry: "As a hen doth gather her chickens, and foldeth them under her wings, so would I gather ye, but ye will not heed."

COMPASSION

IF HUMAN life with all its bitter experiences hath not yet taught you Compassion's first sweet law, hath not yet awakened true discrimination from its long sleep, attaining to knowledge of hidden things will be a curse past telling.

THE CROSS OF FIRE

WOULD you shut your hearts against me that I may not enter in and bless you? Then turn away from him who seeketh you in time of need.

Since Fohat[1] crossed the Circle with his flaming torch hath Life called unto Life for sustenance — support in time of stress. The law which drove that mighty Angel forth to cross one line of life upon another, will drive you back to nothingness, if you persist in flouting it.

---

[1] *Fohat* — the essence of cosmic electricity; the *driving* power of the universe; the universal propelling vital force, at once the propeller and the resultant.

THINE OWN

SEEST thou not, O son of man, thou dost create the good thou believest in with thine whole heart, even as thou dost crush the good thou doubtest? How then canst thou cry "unjust" when evil obstructs thine own path to the footstool of the Gods, and good removes all obstructions from thy brother's path? Thine own will someday meet thine eyes as truly as the morrow's sun will grace the heavenly vault.

ILLUSION'S FLAMES

A CHILD may not play with Rakshasa's[1] flames and go unscathed; the false light of the fires which that Demon doth kindle and flash into human eyes, doth but serve to hide the mouth of a yawning pit.

Better far the steady light of the Sun, though its beams pierce the heart of thine eye, and cause anguish unspeakable. In the one instance, there followeth growth; in the other, destruction.

Many bodies, heads, hands and feet, hath the great Temple of Man, but only one heart. Woe to the hand that strikes at that heart; woe to the foot that tripping, overturns the body.

THE SOUL'S OPPORTUNITY

MY CHILD, what cause hast thou for wreaking vengeance upon that soul which refuses to gain its experience by means of thy travail? Knowest thou not if thou dost rob that soul of its opportunity to suffer and thereby gain the strength to conquer its enemies, thou dost place thyself irrevocably in its power?

The man thou hast sinned against becomes thy Master, and thou must serve him till the debt is paid in full.

The man thou constrainest to travel the path marked out for thee alone, must needs obstruct that path to thine undoing.

---

[1] *Rakshasas* (*Sanskrit*, "raw eaters") — evil spirits and demons in Hindu mythology.

THE VOICE OF GOD

THOU sayest, "God spake to Man in the olden days, man listened and was blessed, but now in the night of Time, God no longer speaks and man is accursed."

Foolish man! God never ceases to speak, but man has destroyed his true sense of hearing by listening too intently to the muffled thunders of the sound waves of human passion pounding against his inner ear.

Seek the Silence, Beloved, and when thou hast found it thou shalt hear again the tender cadences, the word of command, the Song of Life, for God is the same today as yesterday, and His voice doth reach to the outermost bounds of Time and Space, and sings in the heart of man.

JEWELS OF LIGHT

UNCUT, unpolished, are the Jewels hid within this casket, which the Lord of Life hath formed from His own heart, and given unto me.

I pray for power to hold me *still* while He doth cut and polish all these gems, that so, one day I may behold His face reflected in their depths, while He is setting them within a crown, to place on mine own head.

LOVE AND HATRED

ALAS that each human Soul must learn for itself that in trifling with the Emotion of love, its energy is wasted and lost irrevocably; that by bartering that holy birthright for transient pleasure, the most direct path to divine Love and Wisdom is choked by poisonous weeds and thorny brambles, or still worse, is left so empty and desolate that the Snake of Hate alone dares venture there to find a dwelling place.

When the fires of Hate awaken and burn in a human heart, all that makes for life and happiness is consumed, and the unhappy Soul, naked and alone, is left gazing at the ashes of a misspent past.

Neither can you drive that human love back into the heart, any more than you can drive the sap back into a tree, the blood back into the veins; the heart would break, the tree and veins would burst from pressure put upon each molecule. In the wider love, the sap is expelled, the blood distributed, Law is fulfilled, Life is more fully manifested, and The Will of God completed.

WHERE IS GOD?

WHERE shall I find God? If I search the heavens and the earth and the waters under the earth, shall I find him?

No! But if thou wilt search the depths of thine own heart, all that thou findest of Love, of Beauty, of Unselfishness — all that thou knowest of Peace and Joy will open the path to God, and show thee the hidden places wherein thou wilt find all thou canst know and understand.

THE PATH IS HARD

IN A SENSE we may say it is the same path that the Master Jesus followed. There is no other Path, no other way to find the true self, save through effort and suffering. When we think of it from an earthly standpoint, it seems pitiful, that poor, weak, human beings should have apparently so little light to guide them on the way, so little of the comfort that it would seem might be theirs; but those of you who have had an opportunity of watching the wealthy or the so-called "well-to-do," those who seem to enjoy all the good things of this life, know that they are often "of all men most miserable." They are using the gauds of earth to dress up their scarred and tainted carcasses, while their souls are often naked and hungry; and that would show you how little the soul can gain from worldly wealth. It is the strain, the stress, the exercise of power, that gives the final victory.

"A chain is only as strong as its weakest link." A human being, an angel, a god, is only as strong as he has gained power to endure the stress; and that power can only be gained through suffering. If there were any other way, I would have told you — for I sorrow in your sorrow, suffer in your suffering; yet I must stand by, even if it be to see you go down into the midst of the flames, and come up again, if it be necessary to your growth. You sometimes blame me for not saving you from sorrow, for not keeping suffering away from you; but my children, I would gladly give you myself, and all that I am, if it would aid you in your development. But you are as I am, of God — and only through the strength of the God within yourselves and the power that you can gain over these adverse conditions will you be enabled to meet and overcome what will be before you in this and in many lives. The effects of suffering are never lost, any more than effort in any direction can be lost. From my soul, I wish I could convey to you the love I feel for you, the desire I have for your advancement; but every Mother knows that if her child is to grow strong, it must walk by itself, it must learn all it knows of physical conditions by pain; and this process continues to the end. Any human being who tries to make you believe that you can gain spiritual growth without passing through "Golgotha" is tilling you an absolute falsehood. But there is no reason why you should not see the beauty, the good, the glory there is in life. It is around you on every side, it is yours to take and use as it seems best to you — always in the right spirit. I would not have you look at the hells of life, but at the heavens which also lie about you."

STAND UP

HAVE the ruling powers of the Cosmos forced thee into the path of the storm, stripped thee of courage and strength and left thee whirling like a top in the midst of the wreckage of life? With the passing of the storm gather up the fragments of strength and courage, and *stand up*; keep thy feet on the ground.

If thou hast stumbled into the quagmire ruled by the three demons, Doubt, Despair, Distrust — that miry waste dividing

Bondage from Liberty — that fathomless gulf into which each soul stumbles when it lets go of the false and reaches out toward the Real; again I say, Stand up. Trouble not thyself about thy rent and miry garments, or that thou seest no hand in sight to drag thee from the mire. Get upon thy feet and stand! Then thou shalt see the hand.

Have mutual, fair-weather friends nosed a trail and set out to chase thy beloved one to cover? Wilt thou join their pack of yelping curs and help to hound him to his death? At the least, thou mayst deaden the trail, if thou canst not stand by his side and thus prove thine own self.

If so be thou hast power to separate the evil from the evil doer, and help to bear the burden of the Christ who lives and suffers in a stricken soul, then thou mayst hold at bay the enemy of man until its strength is broken, the striken soul is freed, and find that thou art thrice a conqueror. Meet then to take and wear the golden key art thou, for thou hast learned the way to stand upright and open wide the door to greater deeds.

Thinkest thou thy Master will by his diviner power, reach forth to pull thee from the mire or from the power of all the hungry pack and set thee down at His right hand by force of arms, to rule o'er those who have come up through all the hells unscathed by fire of sin? Art thou then such an imbecile as to believe that thine own unbelief, thy fierce repudiation of former faith in Him thou once didst own as Master, will obliterate that Master from the screen of all thy lives? If so it be, then thou art blind indeed; lost, and helpless, or thou hast bound thine eyes and thrown away the crutch: lame and halt, thou now art caught in the morass with only a poor sodden stick of egotistic pride to lean upon; a stick that will surely snap in twain at the first effort to bear thy weight thereon.

Stand up, stretch out thine hand toward the further side of the gulf of thy present delusion, child of the Sun; even if thou canst not yet see that other hand awaiting thine. Bear down on the earth with thine own feet; raise thy head and stand upright.

THE GIFT OF GOD

HE WHO accepteth Me shall live by Me; he who lives by life shall dwell with Mine; and in the Light where dwelleth Mine the heart of God doth pulse unceasingly.

The shade that falls where God doth walk but fills a background drear against which all the light and glory of the Coming Age doth beat in never ceasing rhythm.

Enter thou that light and fold thy wings and rest, thou Bird of Life; thy pinions are Mine own, My Little Ones, to whom I gave Myself, and giving found Myself.

THE BOOK

THOU callest it a brain. I call it a book, into which thou hast writ at command, the records of many lives. As leaf after leaf of that book is turned, as the cycles come and go, I see exposed the tales inscribed in blood wrung from thine own and other hearts. Short sentences illumined with the transitory colors that transient joy hath mixed and given unto thee; whole pages bordered deep with black, o'er which dark shadows seem to flit at will so fast and thick there is no space or chance for written words. Here and there I see a paragraph of careless jest, or record of some kindly deed; and close upon the page where one day *Finis* is to be inscribed by other hands than thine, are other pages where the lines no longer traverse straight across the page from side to side. Uneven are they, and the words run one into the other, and every letter shows the work of aged, trembling hands.

No beauty have those pages to the critic's eye; yet, to the eye of God they are of all most beautiful; for in between those crooked lines and wavering letter strokes, invisible to all but Him, are writ the sum of all the past experience, the mathematics of the soul, that He alone can read and understand.

THE HEIGHTS OF LIFE

WHEN thou hast reached the utmost height of loneliness — that height so far above the Sun-kissed hills, the softly shaded valleys where once you dreamed away the time in blissful introspection and have left behind you all that sensuous life had folded close, the human love, delights of eye and ear, and tender touch of helpful hand — 'twill seem the very heavens have fallen, the earth rejected and thee cast forth condemned. Thy soul will seem suspended in the depths apart from all created things, dead, as though the icy blast of winter's storm had wrapped it all about; alive, as though volcanic fires were eating into every quickening cell. The formless, soundless pressure of illimitable Space will beat upon your ears, and all the light of all the Suns in Space will sear your eyes; until at last, the debt of sentient life repaid, you yield submissively and cry, "God save me from the desolation, the utter loneliness of all created things, and let me lose myself in Thee alone."

No tongue or pen can tell what then befalls that naked Soul, stripped of its gauds — the things which weighed it down, and chained it to a rocky waste: for, losing all it held in memory fond, it finds itself at last, alive with God's own life; a part of every tree and flower, at one with every living thing; a tone of all the melodies the swinging stars give forth — a light which lightens Earth and Sea and Sky, the hosts of Angels and the Cherubim.[1] All, all in thee, and thou in God.

FIND THE GOOD

DEEP indeed thy poverty, thou son or daughter of the Shadow, when for thine own sustenance thou filchest from thy brethren that which they would gladly part with for the asking — the evil tilings of long ago that they would kill and bury.

---

[1] *Cherubim* (*Hebrew*) — in Christianity, an order of angels who are watchers. *Genesis* places Cherubim to guard the lost Eden, and the Old Testament frequently refers to them as guardians of the divine glory.

Long and hard will be the lesson thou must learn ere Wisdom can enfold thee with her mantle and show thee how much wiser it had been for thee to search for all the Godlike qualities concealed within thy brother's heart, that thou might be partaker with him in the blessings so revealed, instead of drawing to thyself and giving power to all the demons he hath lulled, to fasten their vile fangs within thy quivering flesh, with all the strength that Tanha[1] gives to evil things. If thou wouldst look with half the will thou givest to the search for evil things, to find the good within the heart of every living thing, how great would be thy recompense, thou starved and weary pilgrim of the nether path.

Things of darkness seek the darkness, and if by dwelling on the evil thou imputest to thy brother, thou dost darken all thy sphere of being, straight as flies the needle to the magnet will fly the demons of the night to thee: and most of all to fear will be this truth that thou wilt see those demons as the angels of the light, so great will be the darkness thou hast made.

THE CALL OF THE FLESH

AH, CHILDREN, children that ye are, in your hunger for the old joys, or the unexplored field of some new experience, ye forget that the old joys were the seed of your present woes, that the new field must inevitably lead you into a morass of similar suffering.

The call of the flesh, the intoxication of the new field, cause you to forget the consequences which in your more enlightened hours you know must follow, though do not always admit it to yourselves. So, inadvertently, or through your craving for something — anything, that will fill the void in your starving hearts, ye reach out for the frothy sweetmeats, the sugared aloes, which bear the semblance of food. If the pain which follows were all, it might be well for you: but alas, it is not all; in tampering with the higher

---

[1] *Tanha (Pali)* — the thirst for life; the desire to live on this earth. This desire is what causes rebirth or reincarnation.

centers of your life you lose your power of spiritual digestion, and in losing that, you have also lost your hunger — the call of your Divinity — and your ability to assimilate the stronger food, which alone could satisfy.

GIVE WAY

GIVE way, thou stolid, selfish miniature of ease, and let the King pass by, or prone upon the earth his knights will strike thee down!

There is no room for thee, no place in all of Labor's fair domains for such as thou.

The King, God's workman, hath no time or will to set thee gently by when on his way to fight the last long battle for the rights of man, which thou and all thy kind, in sloth, in revelry and lust have forced upon Him and the land which gave thee birth. Give way or die.

THE GIFT OF LIFE

How hard it seemeth, ye who take no note of Nature's loveliest moods — to learn the lesson taught by every curving stem of flower and leaf — to bend, when thou must face the tempest and the storms of life; and so protect that part of thee, thy face, thy features, that which marks thy character, and proves to every seeing eye thy fitness for the gift of Life.

The tree which reacheth toward the heavens in straight unbending line is but support for all the foliage and the seed; while curved and straight lines, stem and tree are needful, the curve which touches close the flower and seed — the finer forms of life — doth give protection and make possible the lives of many, while the straight, unbending line is One, alone.

THY CROWN

THE Prince is not the King; then how can ye in justice crown the Prince and leave the King uncrowned?

Know ye not the crown doth symbolize all power, and when ye build an image of that power and place it on the brow of Him ye call your Lord, ye rob the King of that which is His due, ye close the path through which all power descends, and make the crown a thing of naught?

Give unto God thyself and all thou hast, and He Himself will set His seal within the crown which He will set upon His firstborn's brow, that so in turn it may descend to thee.

But think ye well before ye ask for that same crown the Prince doth wear. Its jeweled front doth flash its brilliant beauty forth on all who look thereon, but he who wears it doth not see that beauty rare; the sharp and jagged edges of the underside, the weight of heavy metal, piercing deep into the flesh and pressing sore the brow; these are His alone — His part of the inheritance within that crown.

THE POWER TO BUILD

"ALL, all I am, my child," the Father saith, "I fain would shower on thee. The fullness, majesty and power of life, in vast immeasurable streams; the wealth and glory of all suns in space — the wisdom garnered by the use of all the higher attributes of gods and men; all, all I hold in trust, I fain would give to thee; and that which I now ask of thee is that with willing heart and in the love which crowns all service pure, thou wilt take up the *little things* of life and do them wisely, gladly — knowing that in giving them to thee to do I give thee power to build and cross the Bridge which must be built by effort of thine own to span the stream 'twixt me and thee."

NO RECALL

THICKEST thou that aught the world can offer could buy back the life that thou of thine own will hast given unto God? Having given that priceless gift — a life — to the service of thy God — the service of thy brethren — thou canst not take it back. That life has entered into the Soul of all and has become a part of every thing and creature — a part of everything that breathes the breath of life. It is no longer thine to give or take away.

It smiles on thee in every rippling brook, in every tender face that lifts itself to thine. It flows from every tear that falls from others' eyes. It throbs in every heart, in every pain of body or of mind. It forms a part of every offered sacrifice. It beats in every measure, every tone, and glows in every sun. Thou mayst befoul the form which holds it, but thou canst not soil the life that is no longer thine, nor rob thy brethren of the gift, for it is theirs, not thine alone, when once accepted by thy God.

THE TRIMURTI

THOU, the Wonderful, the Trimurti, Brahma, Vishnu, and Shiva,[1] hast now revealed to thy servant a mystery:

The Firstborn son of the God of War hath passed from his Father's side between the wings of the Great Bird Garuda[2] — the Bird whose talons wield the thunderbolts of Heaven — to the back of the Eagle of the Western mountains. In swift flight shall the Eagle bear the Great Deliverer, for whom our eyes have long waited, to Aryan[3] skies where, standing upright on the Bird's left

---

[1] *Trimurti* (*Sanskrit*, "three faces") — the Trinity in Hinduism, consisting of Brahma, the creator, Vishnu, the preserver, and Shiva, the destroyer.
[2] *Garuda* (*Sanskrit*) — a gigantic bird, a half-eagle and half-man, which served as a steed for Vishnu. Esoterically, it is the symbol of the great Cycle.
[3] *Aryans* — the people of India. The ancient name of Northern India was *Aryavarta* (*Sanskrit*, "land of Aryans").

wing, he shall re-establish the Lunar Dynasty[1] and bring peace and plenty to a people oppressed.

When the Rivers of the far East and the West meet and commingle, then shall the God of War bury the seven-tipped arrows he now holdeth in hand, beneath the Ocean so formed, and a mighty Race again rule the Earth.

THE DEAD IN LIFE

FIT food are ye for the astral vultures that feed upon you, for dead ye are, while yet ye live.

Swollen, besotted with pride, accursed of God, the fiends ye have called from the depths look on you with horror. Fattened by the blood of the human hearts ye break, ye loll at ease, and not only refuse to enter the light of life yourselves, but bar the way to that light, that others may fall in the darkness ye create. Your lying tongues and deceitful ways cause the weak to stumble and go down to death. Fools that ye are, do you think in your blindness the law is dead?

THE PRICE OF LOVE

TO THE SOUL with the capacity for a great love there will some time come a moment of illumination, a moment of divine intuition when the veil between spirit and matter is temporarily lifted and that soul catches a glimpse of the tragedy which lies concealed behind the present rapture and dimly senses the icy chill of its approach.

So it must ever be, for every great love bears the seed of a deep tragedy. Such love is seldom understood or appreciated at its full value, and still more seldom is it returned in kind.

In the moment of illumination the soul realizes beyond all doubt that the shadow of vicarious atonement, of sacrifice past telling, awaits it also as it has awaited every divinely inspired soul

---

[1] *Lunar Dynasty* — in Hinduism, a legendary dynasty that descended from the moon. Krishna belonged to one of the branches of this dynasty.

since time for man began. But the veil drops quickly, the momentary revolt against undeserved suffering is stilled. Love sheds its radiant beams over all common things, dazzling the intellect, and magically endowing the beloved one with all the attributes of a God. And so self-crowned with the diadem of sacrifice, the soul passes on to its Gethsemane[1] and Golgotha[2] to pay the price demanded by divine law for bestowing upon a mortal that which belongs alone to God.

JUSTICE REIGNS

"All's well! All's well!" loudly calls the watchman at the gate. "Sleep on, sleep on, ye kings, and lords, and princes all, and take your rest.

"Huzza! Huzza! Fill up your glasses to the brim. Drink deep of pleasure's draught, ye sons and daughters of my lords, nor fail to satisfy each lust of eye and mind.

"No need of care have ye, for am not I, your slave, erstwhile in bond to want, now watchman at the gate, and watcher over yon?

"Ye fools, and blind of soul, ye saw no thirst for vengeance in mine eye. Ye heard no cry for justice from my lips so stiff with pain, on that foul day when first ye brought me under thrall to you.

"Now, even while ye sleep or revel, I your watchman and your slave, will lay the train and light the fuse of righteousness for man.

"I, even I, will open wide the gate and let the people in — the broken, spoiled, enslaved and sore tried common people of the slums whom ye have kept without the gate. Ye could not spoil them of their love of life, though all things else worthwhile lay in your grasp; and love of life hath opened wide the eyes once sealed by want, to see the writing on the wall. The day of weighing cometh nigh, and ye must stand upon the scales.

---

[1] *Gethsemane* — the garden in Jerusalem where Jesus Christ was betrayed.
[2] *Golgotha* — a hill, also known as Calvary, outside Jerusalem where Jesus Christ was crucified.

"All's well! All's well! Sleep on, my lords and princes, or revel as ye will. I, the slave whom ye by indolence or wrong have robbed of virtue, manhood, innocence, am given ward o'er you.

"Sleep on and revel, fathers, sons and daughters now within the gates, till strikes the hour before the dawn. Then shall ye wake, in deed and in truth, to learn that justice reigns."

LISTEN

Soul of My Soul, Heart of My Heart, bend down thine ear, and listen thou well. Listen, as listens a mother, who, with smile on her lips and light in her eyes, lists to the beat of the fast coming feet that are bringing her loved ones, her husband or children, back to their hearthstone — back to her arms.

Listen, and know that the heartthrob thou feelest, the life-pulse thou hearest, is but the extension, the rhythmic revealing of heartthrob and life-pulse arising in me, escaping fast from me, and finding a shelter in thy willing heart, till thou sendest them forth on their mission of service, it may be to people a world through the love they invoke, or empty a world through the hatred they bear.

I am the Ultimo,[1] thou the revealer, and also dispenser. In thee lies the power to turn into channels of Good, or to poison with Evil the love-stream that flows from my soul to thine own.

Child of Eternity! Seek well and listen! List till the rhythmic vibration, the life-beat of God, strikes thine ear.

THUS SAITH THE LORD

Thus saith the Lord — my Lord to me: Open thine eyes and behold my face. Thou hast looked too long at my bleeding feet and rememberest not the smile on my face. Thou hast looked too long at the dire effects, and not enough at the causes of sin. Thou hast wept and prayed o'er and fondled and cherished the long secret sins thou wilt not let go.

---

[1] *Ultimo* (*Latin*) — the last.

Thou fearest the Law, that Law which is mine, which is me and is thee, and in fearing, thou losest the light of my love, that love which o'ertops and enhances the Law, as this one little sphere is o'ertopped and enhanced by the heavens which surround it — by limitless space.

Look up, my child, from my feet to my face.

THE CHRIST-BORN

Scarred and broken on the wheel of the Dark Star, beset by all the wiles of man, and tried by demons fierce — the Dragon's blood ye drank to quench the Tanha thirst hath now been turned to living water in your breast, and all who come to you in faith shall drink and live.

Rejoice that ye have kept your troth with Christ — for He will turn that water into precious wine when comes the last great change, and clothe you with a garment white as wool, that ne'er hath borne a stain.

THY TRUST

Royal prince of the Kingdom of God, Son of thy Father, the Thrice-born! Great indeed is thy station, immeasurable the power that waits upon thy crowning — thy foot upon the dais of thy Father's Throne.

In the shadow of Infinity thou standest, Son of Suns, unknowing of thy future, all thy past unknown to thee.

Thy serfs and vassals — thy passions and desires — now press thee close and plead for grace that thou hast power to grant or hinder.

Yet, notwithstanding rank and station, there is not a slave or minion in thy Father's Kingdom so poor as now thou art, if thou art recreant to thy trust. No thief locked in thy castle dungeon can be so hideous in thy sight as thou wilt be if thou art traitor in the sight of those to whom thy heart, in faith, was turned, when all the world was young to thee — when purity of motive, purpose, soul looked squarely out from eyes that never wavered when they met the eyes of those who loved and trusted them.

A little thing it seemed, when, midst the glamor, clanging bells and great rejoicing on that day which ushered in maturity for thee, thy Father gave His lance and signet ring to thee, and bade thee hold the outer Temple Gate, that so no enemy might gain the inner Wall — that Guardian Wall, each stone of which is chiseled and cemented by the brawn and blood of countless races of mankind — that Wall which guards the greatest treasure of His Kingdom, the holiest of Holy Things — the Sacred Fire, which, lit by God's own Hand, has never since been quenched.

Art thou a traitor, thou, the Son of Kings? Is thine the hand that pierced the Wall and led the foe within?

If so it be, thrice traitor then art thou. Thy Father's signet ring, thy Mother's bed, the Holy Fire — all jeopardized by thee.

Each stone that fell through cause of thine will cry for vengeance from the ground it touched.

By king or beggar, prince or slave, a trust betrayed is all the same, and bringeth recompense in full.

Art thou thy Father's firstborn, His beloved Son?

Then stand behind His Throne. Sharpen thy sword if it hath rusty grown, and keep it drawn. That Throne is thine, and thou must hold it in the days to come. As thou defendest it, so shall it be thine own defense, when kingdoms fall like rain, and men in terror flee.

THE WORKSHOP

"Come apart with me, thou child of my begetting. Come apart from all the noisy crowd. Come from under the weight of man's infirmities and sins. Come away from the path of the flood of women's tears, the pressure of helpless children's cries, those cries which beat unceasingly upon the ears of tender souls.

"Come thou with Me into the cleft of yonder rock; lie down and rest, and I will show thee wondrous things which thou mayest bring to pass on earth, if so thou wilt." Thus spake the Christ.

"Behold the city of a thousand hills — a city white and glorious, and in the midst thereof see thou the poor in spirit, the lame, the halt, the blind, the castaways of all the earths the cyclic sweep of Time hath gathered up. And over all the mighty throng, like outspread wings above a nest, see thou the peace of God, the glory shining from His face and sweeping o'er and o'er each worn and battered form, until that form is lost within the glory to appear again like unto God.

"Then see thou One in simple majesty of form who saith unto the throng about Him: 'Listen, children of my soul! Lo, ye have suffered, labored, danced and played these many years on earth, whence ye are now released. While under glamor of the Jinns ye have believed that ye were laboring hard and sore bestead — but now with Me get ye unto your work — the work of Gods and Angels.

"'The glory and the peace that ye have won with Me must be transferred to earth and we must do the mighty work. Breathe deep and fill your hearts, arid by the strands of Love we weave thereof, descend to earth swiftly, silently seek out the rich, the powerful, the great, the sorely tempted, blind and halt and lame of soul who know not yet how poor they are, and, throwing off our breastplates, set free the streams of Love and Peace and Glory within our hearts, for sore indeed is now their need.

"'The earth will change. There will be no more sea. Heaven will be brought to earth, the twain be merged in one, and then at last Love will be justified, its will be done when we have loosed the chains which bind the souls of men.'

"All this will I show thee when thou comest apart with Me, for know ye now that Heaven is the Workshop of the Gods, and earth the playground of the Jinns.

"Man must make his Heaven, if he would dwell therein, and he can only make it as he worketh day by day with Me, apart from all, yet one with all." Thus spake the Christ.

THE INTERVALS OF LIFE

LOOK for the secrets contained in the intervals.
The sounded notes plainly tell their stories to the listening ear, but what man hath sounded the deeply hidden mysteries of the rests between those notes?

Bury the past. Open the door of the future that the resurrected may improve the present opportunity.

Life's mysteries are only mysterious to the deaf and blind.

The mind of God is mirrored in the mind of man, and he who would know God must first know man.

Individual man is the tool, Life is the Master workman now building the Universal Temple. The stones for its building are the divine principles carved by the hand of God, and the mortar for their laying is wet by the tears of the human race. Not until the Temple is complete will stone and tool attain to consciousness of the glory to be revealed in them.

In all the literature of the world there is naught so supremely selfish, in the highest acceptance of the term, as are the exhortations of the Beatitudes.[1] In praying for those who despitefully use you and persecute you, you are praying for yourself, for the sinner and the sinned against are one in the Christ to whom appeal is made. The merciful, the pure in heart, are each yourself; you are the blessed, yours the reward. You cannot separate yourself from your brother self. You can neither pray for, bless or curse one without the other. Yet must you pray and bless and work, or die the death of the unregenerate.

"I HAVE KEPT THE FAITH"

BEATS there a heart so callous, so unresponsive as to feel no thrill of courage, no feeling of gratitude that it belongs to the same grade of substance, beats to the same measure as that which

---

[1] *Beatitudes* — blessings made by Jesus Christ in the Sermon on the Mount (see Matthew 5:3–12) and in the Sermon on the Plain (see Luke 6:20–23).

enveloped the man and prompted the words of the dying Paul: "I have kept the faith"?

What would be the result if the Higher Self of each one called upon us to make a similar assertion in the hearing of a waiting multitude, after years of such trial as Paul endured for his "faith's sake"?

And what is this faith which Paul once defined as "the substance of things hoped for"?

The answer comes from the heart of all things and wells up from our own hearts to our lips, "It is the life of our life — the one attribute — the basic principle of all our hopes, fears, longings and possibilities. Without it we were the most forlorn, helpless and hopeless creatures in the wide universe."

When all we have loved, trusted, worked for, prayed for, endured for, leaves us someday in the midst of one of the fiercest storms of trial; when it seems as though the very foundations of the world were giving away and we were plunging into the depth of Hades; out from some inner shrine, some holy place, where God is dwelling in fullness for the time being, there comes a soft whisper to our inner ear, bringing in its wake a wave of hope and courage which stirs some stagnant, long-neglected deep of our nature and sets it into rapidly pulsating motion; and then into our hearts and heads is wafted the message: "Be of good cheer, I have overcome."

"Overcome what? And by what?" questions the lower mind.

Clear cut and sharp comes the answer: "Overcome the world and all that is in it that is antagonistic to the highest good and overcome it by the power of Faith." Faith sees the first step of the long ladder we must climb, and then glances along the other steps and says to us: "Take that first step and the rest will be easy"; faith that looks into the heavens of a starlit night and says: "Even as the hand of Infinity holds those worlds in equilibrium, as century after century they traverse unending spaces, so will that same hand hold this little world which constitutes my individual self, so I have no occasion to fear. All I need is power to will and work — the Infinite Father will do the rest. Faith walks by one's side, even if its face be veiled, as we stumble down the dark valley of death and through hells beneath — those hells that have quenched the fires of hope, of love, of mercy, of even desire for existence — and says: "Look up, beloved, this is not all of life; take me, use me as a shield against the darts of the devils that haunt this place, and fight thy way out." And, listening to that plea and obeying it, we find the way-opening before us; we find the devils were either powerless to injure us or that they were unsubstantial, transitory, dream figures which melt away before our eyes, as step by step we advance, covered by that shield of Faith.

Aye, Faith is indeed the life of our life, the impulse to every worthy action; the basis of every invention, every scientific discovery, every advance in all fields of life; and more than all else to the longing, soul-starved human being hopeless of ever being understood by or ever gaining a place in the hearts of those it loves and serves, and overcome with a horrible fear of death, and even worse fear of continued life.

What words can picture the return of a lost faith to such an one?

Dwelling on all these truths, can we not imagine with what wholesome pride came the words: "I have kept the faith," from the lips of that old, worn-out, dying man; worn-out in the service of his fellowmen and the Christ he loved?

Who would not reverently repeat the same words to himself and pray that he too might be able to utter them in a like hour of supreme trial, in the same spirit and with the same power?

The greatest Initiate,[1] the humblest slave may have a right to utter them; and in the utterance the two would be made one in the heart of Infinite Love.

---

[1] *Initiate* — the designation of anyone who was received into and had revealed to him the mysteries and secrets of Nature.

OPEN THINE EYES

Open thine eyes — the eyes of thy Soul — poor, fickle, changeable atom of man that thou art, lest thou blindly enter again and again the flames of the nether fires, when the free, glad fields of Elysian[1] bliss are thine for thy Willing and Seeking.

Knowest thou not that the loyal service of thy friend to even that which seemeth error unto thee, will bring that friend, and thee with him (if so be that thou art true), unswervingly to righteous principle; for loyalty to aught that God hath made, whatever be the name that man bestows upon it, will bring thee surely, safely to the heart of God, though dark and devious be the paths thy feet doth tread to reach that heart.

Never canst thou reach thy goal, the goal where God in Christ doth dwell eternally, if false to thine own soul. And false thou art if false unto thy brethren.

Even though a seeming Christ in form shouldst come to thee and say, "Come unto me and sit henceforth on my right hand, though in the coming, I must bid thee crush the hearts of these thy brethren underfoot," I say to thee: Beware! Not so doth come the Christ. But Satan in the guise of Christ might well deceive thee, if it be that thou hast never known that God cannot belie Himself. God in Truth, is Truth sublime, and Truth is Loyalty, before, above, beyond, all other attributes.

If thou dost deem thy brother sore deceived, be brave enough to walk upright, unwavering, by that brother's side till thou hast led him into what is Light to thee, or through the paths of pain that thou hast walked with him, perchance thou shaft learn that he held the Light and thou wert in the shadow. Only so can Christ the Master come to thee and offer thee in truth a place at his right hand.

---

[1] *Elysium* or *Elysian fields* — a paradise in Greek mythology.

THE LIVING CHRIST

Poor, striken soul, that needs must lay thy crucified — thy Christ — within a sepulcher and seal the door, while yet some other soul hath sought and found the Christ alive. Alive in every tree and flower, in beast and bird as well as in the human heart, where, in thine ignorance, thou now wouldst fain confine Him, in fear that Christ might be degraded by too close a contact with the lesser souls which truly He alone could ever bring to life and being.

Stricken sore indeed is he who in his selfish sorrow for the Christ who died, his worship of all funeral trappings, doth fail to see the living Christ in every thing and creature, as well as in the heart of every earnest seeker for the truth, who undertakes his search to still the yearning cry within his soul for sight or sound of that which, from the inmost recesses of human life, is ever drawing all Its own to recognition of Itself.

There is no rest, no peace for such a stricken one until the great reality beyond all seeming comes to birth within himself, and sets him free to seek wherever Truth doth lead, e'en though it be through all the fires of Hell or to the very gates of Heaven. For where the Christ hath gone, all men may go, upheld and comforted by the same love that hath sustained and comforted each seeker for the Grail since time for man began.

JUSTICE

The Stars are now rocking with the tread of the vast army of Souls who are coming from far-off fields of Hadean[1] darkness to demand of you, of me, of all the races of mankind, speedy release from the weight of the fiery chains they have been loaded with; surcease from the anguish they are now enduring because of our refusal or neglect to profit by their martyrdom, when they, in love, have lain their torn and mangled bodies down upon the earth that we might step thereon to reach with ease a higher round of

---
[1] *Hadean* (from *Hades*, the Greek god of the underworld, and the underworld itself) — infernal or hellish.

the Cosmic ladder, and so open the gates which now shut them out of Heaven.

Vengeance for outraged love has been the burden of the loud wail that has shaken the foundations of the earth for ages gone.

"Vengeance is mine," answers the Lord our God, "And I am love."

Out from the midst of the great White Throne comes the command, "Open wide the Star strewn vaults of the Heavens, ye Angels of the Gates, and let the victims of man's inhumanity pass through to behold the administration of long defeated justice."

"MY FATHER"

WHEN the storm center of thy life is stirred, to its focal point and thy whole being is dissolved in the mighty thought waves which sweep unchecked to the boundaries set by thine own soul; when from amidst the roar and tumult of thy clashing thoughts, there comes a low, gasping, shuddering, "Father, hear me, save me," thinkest thou thy Father will fail to recognize the tones of thy voice amidst the myriad voices assailing His ears and so will pass thee by unheeding? Ah, thou little knowest: Couldst thy Mother's ear be deceived in the voice of her child? Would it matter to her what name thou gavest her? Whether thou cryest in pain or in joy? Would not soul reach soul unhampered by other earthly sounds at the first sound of thy voice?

Then why shouldst thou doubt that thy Father is more able to hear the voice of His child, whether thou callest Him Jehovah[1] or God, Zeus[2] or Jupiter?[3]

The name thou now bearest will die with thee, but thine own name, thy true name, is graven on the hands and in the heart of thy Father in Heaven, and though thy Father's name has never passed

---

[1] *Jehovah* — a Hebrew name for the God of Israel.
[2] *Zeus* (*Greek*) — the Father of the Gods in Greek mythology.
[3] *Jupiter* (*Latin*) — the ancient Roman God of Heaven, daylight, thunder; the Father of all the Gods; the Supreme Deity of the Romans, identified with the Greek Zeus.

the lips of mortal man, that name is graven in thine own heart, and that heart, unconsciously mayhap to thee, cries out that name when it prompts thee to say, "My Father."

THE WEAPONS OF THE SELF-BORN

AH, "LITTLE ONE," thou child of the long travail of the Christs, how weak thy struggle, how unfitted art thou for the battle with the powers of evil now arrayed against thee!

Unwitting of the methods of thy forbears — they who fought the Dragon with its own sharp claws and slew it past all hope of resurrection — thou hast yet but learned to grasp such weapons as they used to crush the crawling worm.

Arouse thyself and seek to slay that Dragon's progeny — the Dragon's teeth sown over all the earth — tenfold more the spawn of Evil than the power which gave them birth.

Wilt thou stand by supine and let them slay the good, the pure, the holy — yea, slay thyself, in this most cruel of the cruel wars that ever devastated dwelling place of man — the war of self 'gainst self?

When all Illusions sensuous coils are wound about thine eyes thine enemy doth seize thy strength to turn the face of Truth, of Holiness and Wisdom to the wall of Sense, and places in their stead the well disguised, the cold and passionless, the craven faces of thy foes, while they would force thee to thy knees in slavish worship of the dead in life.

Arouse thee, child though now thou art, unbind thine eyes, and even in the time a sunbeam takes to strike the earth, the weapons of the Self-born shall descend to thee and thou shalt tear those evil faces from the wall and bring again to light the hidden faces of the Gods of Truth, of Justice, Love and Wisdom.

THE GREATEST IS CHARITY

"But the greatest of these is Charity." Charity which covers a multitude of sins, the charity which recognizes and accepts responsibility for the man or woman in the depths of degradation, as at least partly due to the vileness of his own imaginings, and the imaginings of every other person who has imputed evil to such an one; for know, ye who prate of possession of the power of suggestion, of hypnotism, of psychic power, that you — you, my brother — if guilty, will answer in the great day of settlement for the condition of that fallen one. If he goes to Hell, you will go with him. Owning to the possession of the power that would have lifted him from the depths into which he had sunk, or had been pushed, mayhap, by the Pharisee[1] who now passes by on the other side, you have let that power lie idle. You — you, my sister, will face the inquisitor by the side of the sister you have despised, the child you have left orphaned, desolate, to the care of the "beasts of the jungles" — "the beasts of mammon," — because its mother and father had not been united by another man's ceremony.

You — you, my sister, my brother, who strip every thread of reputation from a weaker brother or sister; you who bring the wolves and jackals of society to tear the flesh — the good name — from the bones of another human being, when in letters of living fire the one word *Charity* looms up before your inner eyes. You see it on altar, transept, and over the entrances of your great temples and churches. The arches or the naves of those temples are trembling from the volume of rich sound from organ and from voice, as they breathe out in song — the theme of Charity.

You who reach out a hand, in your poverty and wretchedness to a sister, a brother, to be fed; and when your craving for material food is satisfied, when the riches of spiritual teachings have poured

---

[1] *Pharisees* (*Hebrew*, "separated") — a Jewish sect, from the 2nd century BCE to the 1st century CE, known for their strict adherence to religious laws and traditions, often characterized by their emphasis on oral law, meticulous observance of rituals and separation from those they considered impious.

out upon you in their fullness, turn and bite the hand that fed you, or pour out the vitals of long suppressed jealousy and rage.

"Charity for me," cry such poor souls, "but the torments of Hell for thee," if thou hast given them charity, and they are not big enough to rest under the weight of kindness.

There is a river broad and deep enough to cover the path of a solar system, the waters of which are pure and sweet and cleansing enough to give life and healing and joy surpassing aught we know; and the name of that river is color carven and jeweled in the sky above, and over all its length and breadth. We call it Consciousness.

Out from its etheric counterpart, in strains past human telling, sounds eternally the echoes of the song of Life.

Enter that river, lie down on its bosom, let its waters pour over and through your soiled and weary bodies.

Drink of it, laugh with it, weep with it; then rise up and go out into the world and hunt for the thirsty, the soiled, the weary, and bring them, too, to the banks of that river.

There on its banks shalt thou find a diadem awaiting thee, and carven deep on the golden circlet, emblazoned with jewels of attainment, shalt thou find the word — Charity — *Love*.

TO MINE OWN

A TRUST I gave to thee, the Escutcheon of thy Father's House, the honor of a line of brave defenders, warriors of old, who hated life if it but interfered a jot with Truth and Justice; who gave their lives without a pang, at the demand of Right.

I bade thee keep that Trust secure from all thy Father's foes and thine. I bade thee seek and find thy brethren in those spheres whence they were driven by the powers of darkness when closed the last fierce struggle 'twixt the White and the Black.

I bade thee see to it, no stain should rest upon thine armor, no rust upon thy sword. I come again to thee to ask that thou shouldst draw that sword, to test its metal, throw off the cloak that hides thine armor that I may judge how thou hast kept the Faith. I bid thee open wide thy vestments that I may feast mine eyes upon the brightness of thy breastplate. The day of *use* draws nigh, and I must try my weapons.

Shall I find thine honor in the dust, thy brethren still in bondage, the glory of thy House departed, through thy faithlessness or weakness? Or shall I find thee staunch and true, one of the unconquerable; find thee still the stainless peer of all thy forbears?

Deep now loudly calls to greater deeps across the waves of human woe. The long expected day of Separation draweth nigh.

Those who are mine will answer "Here" when sounds the rallying cry. Those who have faithlessly given their troth to another must go to that other.

The Gage of the mighty in power of today has been flung in the faces of the Warriors of Light, and the battle of Right against Might is on.

PRAYER

REACH down, lost soul though thou be, thou who deniest the source of thy life, thou who hast forgotten thine ancestry, thou who hast flung thy younger brother into the pit thine own desire hath dug, and filched from him his heritage for thine own glory. Thou who hast made a playground of thy Father's heart, and watered the seeds of thine own decay with thy Mother's tears.

Thou who thinkest there is no eye of God to see the bastard forms thou hast created; no ear of God to hear the blasphemous ribaldry with which thou hast polluted the air thou must breathe.

Reach down, lost soul though thou be, beneath the trough of the rolling wave of thine earthly passion, and search for the light of the Christ which even yet shines in thee. Make a path through that wave by Faith,, that the light may pass through to search out thine heart, and — fall on thy knees!

To him who saith to thee, "There is no God to listen to thy mouthings," do thou as I hid thee, fling back the foul lie in his face, for lie it is.

No soul hath ever lifted its voice in prayer for succor in its hour of peril that hath been turned back upon itself.

The foulest wrong one soul may do unto another is to rob it of its faith in God.

Pray unceasingly, but not as one without hope. Pray in praise, in certainty that there are ears to hear, e'en though they be not molded on the pattern of thine own, e'en though the answer to thy prayer doth tarry till the water from the well of life hath overflowed its rim and once more filled the shrunken tissues of thy soul, and washed away all stain of sin, that so the fiery streams of Love Divine now held in leash by that one Christly gleam within thy soul, may egress find to utterly destroy all that lies between thy God and thee, between thee and the Ocean of all Life.

FRIENDSHIP

DESPITE the coldness and the apathy, the cruelty and indifference of many units of humanity toward each other, there are friendships still among them so fine, so rare and pure, that even words would cast a shade upon them; friends so rich in priceless treasures of the heart, that every glance of eye or touch of hand beheld by alien eyes begets an urge towards God, however far the alien feet have wandered from the path.

Narrow trails 'twixt heaven and earth such friendships are. One need only glimpse their loveliness to feel the call to walk therein, mayhap to find the greatest friend of man — the Christ — Who waits the ending of each trail of purity and love.

Rich past human tongue to tell is he who hath a Friend. Neither death, nor heaven, nor hell hath power to sever such a tie. The breath of God hath bound the two in one, and naught can break that bond, however hard the strain upon it be.

Make thyself worthy of a friend, if thou art friendless now, and somewhere on earth that friend will wait thy call. For as the sun doth draw the water from a brook, so shall thy worthiness for friendship draw thy friend to thee at last.

HEARKEN TO ME

HEARKEN, ye children of the New Dispensation! The time is near at hand when He who is to come will reappear among men for the unification of the races of the earth. Open your eyes that they may see. Open your ears that they may hear. And open your hearts that the Son of Man may have place to lay his head, lest He pass you by and ye know him not.

LIFT UP THINE EYES

LIFT up thine eyes, O man, O little man. Lift up thine eyes that so thou mayest behold the Angels of the spheres; the Holy Ones who rode the crest of fiery billows set in motion by the Sons of Flame long ere a thought of thee had crossed the mind of God.

Look up, that so perchance thou mayest catch the pitying glances cast on this Dark Star in passing, by those angel hosts.

Tied to the same wheel of life as thou, yet tied by their own will, midway between the heavens and earth they circle round to hold in equilibrium the lesser worlds which otherwise would be unbalanced.

No need have they to veil their eyes.

Full in the faces of the glorious suns they look, their eyes untroubled, unashamed by aught that meets those mirrored depths.

Messengers are they 'twixt Gods and men and this the message now they bring to thee: "Lift up thy face, O man, to whom the gods gave hands in place of paws; the gods who set thee on thy feet and lifted up thy head, the gods who loosed the cords that bound thy face to earth."

"Lift up thy face, and even shouldst thou read rebuke in those most holy eyes when they shall meet thine own, there also wilt thou find the promise of release when in the days to come thy feet shall also be unbound, and naught have power to hold thee longer to the earth."

THE GUERDON OR THE LOSS

HAVE the Demons of Cowardice, Indolence and Self-aggrandizement seized and bound thee fast, thou child of the Dawn?

Art thou held in thrall by the children of Night — and fain would now escape? Then would I bid thee loudly call upon the Brothers of the fire mist to burn the cords that bind thee fast and set thee free to take thy place amidst the Warriors of the Light.

Dull well thou knoweth that the guerdon of a battle nobly fought can never fall to renegade or leech, so hold thee still until thy bonds are burned if thou wouldst fight to win.

No soldier — chela[1] — of the Mysteries[2] will leave his comrades to the beasts of prey which lurk amidst the shadows of the army's rear he hath been set to guard, and rim for safety to the demons of those shadowy wilds. The proven chela seeks the thickest of the fight and there remains, within his Captain's call, till victory comes.

He who would eat the bread and drink the water portioned to his army corps in time of peace, then climb to safety o'er the dead he had betrayed while still the battle cry was sounding in his ears could never win the crown of life; the Sword of Power.

SING SOFT AND LOW

SING soft and low, ye happy, hopeful, helpful hearts — ye hearts that feel the first faint throb of that strong life-beat pulsing through the unborn child — the new humanity.

Sing soft and low. Not yet the time for swelling notes of victory. Sing, for sing ye must, and never cease from singing. The child

---
[1] *Chela* (*Sanskrit*, "servant") — a disciple.
[2] *Mysteries* — celebrations of initiation and observances, generally kept secret from the profane and uninitiated, in which the origin of things, the nature of the human spirit, its relation to the body, and the method of its purification and restoration to higher life were taught by dramatic representation and other methods.

is now conceived; the birth pangs even now are surging through the Mother Soul, and tho' the travail be most hard and long, the end is even now in sight.

Unto God and thee another Son, another King will come to rule in majesty and power.

Creep away into the dens the underworld doth hold, ye drawers of the waters from the wells of women's eyes, ye who dig deep furrows in the faces of the men who suffer for your sins; for there will be no place for those who weep in that new age, and ye must weep the measure of the tears ye now are drawing from the eyes of those who love and serve you well.

Speak to your hearts, speak low the words of peace and patience, ye who suffer now, and gain endurance through your pain.

Ye well may leave all judgments to the law, for yours will be the prize, yours the honor of the banner bearer through the march of centuries to come.

THE LATCH

Lift up the latch, child of my love, the latch to the door of thy Father's heart: the door of that home thou hast left in rebellion to wander afar into darkness and squalor, in want and in sorrow: left it to seek, yet always to miss, the peace of fulfillment, the joy of attainment.

Dost thou remember, son of my sun, when thy thoughts wander homeward, that only in seeming that latch closed the door; remember that inside the door was no latch and no fastening, and he who would enter had only to stoop to the latch hanging downward, lift it and enter the door of his home?

If a child willed to enter a touch of his finger would lift high the latch, the door would swing open, a face there would meet him; wide open arms would enfold him, and bring him perforce back again to his own.

So now hangs the latch to the door of my heart, but of thine own free will must thou lift it to enter.

THOU HAST DONE WELL

CLOSE the door, my child, shut out the sin, the shame and sorrow. Close the door, for all who enter here touch holy ground.

All sad todays and yesterdays are lost in the tomorrows of the souls that enter here, and all the brightness of the days between is here before thee, waiting here for thee. All of good that thou hast ever lost, all recompense for pain, is here: so close the door, my child, and come into thine own.

Close the door. I would not bid thee come to me and close the way to thy return, did I not know thy duty done — the prize of all fulfillment won by thee.

That which now remains, between thee and the goal thou long hast sought is just the open door, thy pity and thy fear forbids thee now to close.

Why lingerest thou? The wail of human woe now falling on thine ear comes not from child of thine, or friend. 'Tis but the wail, the torturing screams of hosts of souls imprisoned by their higher selves for sins 'gainst thee and me and all the human race.

Thou wilt not? Thou desirest still to stay amidst the lost when joy and peace are thine just for the taking? Thou sayest Heaven would not be Heaven for thee if memory of the cries of the condemned remained with thee.

So be it! Thou hast chosen well; for all the aisles of Heaven, through all eternity, would echo and re-echo all its cries, if but a single soul were left in Hell, on that great day when are recalled by God, the sons He once sent forth to do his bidding. And it is best for thee that thou hast chosen to remain in chains of flesh if so be thou mayest hasten that great day by helping up some weaker soul than thine; some soul that fell and could not rise alone, and by its fall had blocked the way for all who followed in its train. Aye, thou hast done well, my child!

THE CENTRAL FLAME

THE nearer the disciple approaches to the Central Flame of the great Initiation Chamber, the keener grows his sensitiveness to the heat of the fire, the stronger is his realization of its power over him. As the tongues of flame search out the tender places of his flesh he sinks back in terror and fain would turn and flee from the face of the fire that has hitherto been his God, even must he fly to the uttermost parts of the universe.

If he have the power to stand still while the dross of his lower self be burned away and he sees his heart's blood splashing the pavement at his feet, all life is changed for him; his former fear and shrinking are lost in an overwhelming love which embraces even the flames whereby he has suffered. With face transfigured and his once gross body now *a* center of radiating light, he steps from the base of the flame into the great Circle of Conservation — Universal Love. He is no longer a stake for demons to fight over, but a man among men, a God among Gods.

FAITHFULNESS

SAY thou to my Children:
Faithfulness to each individual Ideal of the Soul of all Things and to Us, as representatives of the Great Lodge, will bring them close to us. But, if they would come still nearer, they must not forget that he who would drink of our cup must needs find it a cup of renunciation and sorrow, as well as of joy unspeakable.

Only by kneeling in the dust of this Scarred old Star can we press our lips to the hem of the Christ-garment — that garment whence cometh the healing, life-giving streams, which alone can wash away the tears from our eyes, the bitterness from our hearts.

We can but grope around in the darkness of material life in our search for that gracious garment — Compassion. But, haply in our groping, our weary hands may suddenly touch the hand of God — the hand that with a wave may throw back the curtain shrouding Infinity, and show us not only the hem, but the whole garment, and our souls shining forth from its pure white folds.

SEARCH

Ah, starved and starving souls, held in leash by fear, while just beyond your present vision is a table set that even Christ might find delight in serving, crying out or smothering the cry for one dear Mother Heart to lay thy head upon!

Riven hearts that pulse with longing for "the feel" of some dear little child!

In agony unspeakable, pain and fever, lie countless stricken ones, hopeless of relief, looking only to the deep, dark stream beyond to drown their suffering, while just above their heads a hand is feeling for their feeble wavering hands to lead them to release. If thou art one of these, hold still, that so that hand may clasp thine own.

Feast and Mother, Child and Healing, Life and Death, all doth lie within the Father's heart, that beats through thine.

Search, and thou shalt find! I who tell thee, tell the true.

"HE COMES"

Ho! Outposts, "Light the signal fires." From Mountaintop along the chain of Hearts which girdle all the world, flash brightly out the long awaited message — the message which till now hath only flickered softly in all lowly places, in the coulees and the quiet valleys where all Nature cries are hushed before the couch of the great World-Mother[1] in the parturition pains which bringeth a Christ to birth.

---

[1] *Mother of the World* — the Greatest Spirit of the Feminine Principle, who stands at the head of the Hierarchy of Light. She has Her personifications in many religions of the world as the Supreme Goddess. The Mother of the World incarnated Herself as Mary to give life to Jesus Christ.

Stretch out thy hand, O man, on either side of thee and take thy brother's hand, in hut, in palace, home or street, and form a close wrought chain through which no jot of all the Love, the Righteousness, the Justice of a new, a greater age may pass and thou wilt find that all the light and glory of the newborn sun will be reflected in thine own glad face.

LIFE IN DEATH

THOU who bearest Death's dark visage, reach out and draw the creatures of Thy will still closer to Thy side, and let them search Thy face, and place their hands within Thy Heart, that so they come upon the secrets of Thy purposes.

No fear of Thee have I, for Thou and I have oft clasped hands in peace, and now I know Thee well for That Thou art — the friend of man.

But these, my children, know Thee not, and I would plead that Thou draw near that they may learn that Life in all its fullness lies within the fastnesses of Thy mysterious Being.

COMPASSION'S VEIL

THE Merciful Law, Compassion's self, hath veiled thine eye, that while thou walkest in the darkness of this nether world thy sight should not be blasted by the glory shining forth from that great soul who bears my message to the dead in life as well as to the dying and the stillborn souls which throng the portal of the inner sphere, and walk unhindered midst the crowds that gather in the paths and byways of all sentient life — the crowds which thou and thine do help to swell.

A robe of common flesh, ungainly form, and countenance that callest not for lust of eye; no beauty hath my Messenger, that thou desirest it. Nor canst thou see until thine inner eye is opened and with reverent hand thou tearest down the evil which hides that soul from thee; and this thou mayest not do, until the Sun of

Life be shining bright within thy heart, for in the darkness, sudden light of radiant soul would blind thine eyes.

In thy sorrow for thy wasted opportunities, thy cruelty, the needless anguish borne in thy behalf, my Messenger would also suffer in thy suffering as ne'er in all its flight from Heaven to earth it hath been called to suffer for other cause than that which tries thy soul; the cause of universal woe — man's disobedience to the law of God.

SHIFT THY LOAD

DOES the load press hard? Is thy shoulder grazed? Thy back bent low? Are thy nerves and muscles tense and strained by the stress of the burden borne? Doth the world woe press thy heart till it seem to burst its leash?

Then, child of my sorrow, shift the load from shoulder to back, from nerve to heart, from heart to shoulder.

The weight is needful, the close bound burden doth hold the ransom and crown of thy soul.

Remember, 'tis always in darkness and silence — in the heavy pressure of our human woe, that the Light of God conceives and brings its own to birth.

So shift thy load, my child, and wait in patience for release until the Law shall set thee free.

At least the shift will give relief, and at the most it may uncover one of Life's most precious mysteries.

DEBTORS TO LIFE

MY SON why callest thou on me for Succor, why plead for Wisdom's gifts, while all unrecognized, forgotten or neglected, lie all the gifts bestowed on thee in answer to thy calls of long past days.

To rid thy conscience of thy debtors' load thou claimest inalienable right to all the Universe holds of good, and base thy claim upon thy kinship with the source of thy frail life.

But Life is Law, and Law gives naught for naught.

He is a thief who takes from Life all that he may and then refuses payment of the debt in kind.

THE SPEECH OF CHRIST

HE WHO would tell thee that the Christ doth speak to him in words, deceives himself and thee.

Not so doth speak the Christ.

By deeds of Love and Justice the Christ must utter Thought if he would speak to man while man is man. By deeds must give the key the Morning Star sounds forth to constellations bright, the hosts of Heaven who sing the Cosmic Symphonies age after age.

Words are impotent to express or voice the thoughts of God, and only man of all created things hath scorned the thoughts expressed in deeds and in their stead hath chosen sound of his own voice in speech to satisfy his soul.

LOYALTY

SPEAK the word soft and low — let the vibrations of each letter of the word sink into the depths of your consciousness. What mental pictures you will find gathering upon the mirror of your soul! Countless precious lives yielded in sacrifice for Christ's sake, on the fiery altars raised to the black demons of human selfishness by the disloyal. Pictures of friends, families, homes, laid on the Holy altars of sacrifice, for Truth's sake, by those who could see naught but a long, lonely path stretching far, far out into a hopeless future; a path which their footsore feet must tread ere they could catch a glimpse of their promised reward.

Pictures of gibbets, scaffolds, the rack, fiery furnaces and the torture chamber; and acres upon acres of unmarked graves — the sepulchers of those who once trod the earth you are treading today, with heads uplifted to the heavens in the hope of the visible descent of the Holy Spirit; with hearts attuned to the keynote struck by God when He called His people at the break of a new day.

Pictures of army after army, in never ending procession marching on to the doom prepared for them by their country's traitors, yet glad to yield up their lives to preserve their nation's honor.

Brokenhearted but yet faithful mothers, wives, sisters, sinking into poverty and evil rather than betray a recreant father, husband or brother to the wild beasts of human law.

Loyalty! Is it surprising that the word falls heavy on our hearts, yet rises in power and volume to immeasurable heights when it reaches the ears of our souls?

When you think of that vast concourse of souls, to any one of which the word *Loyal* may be fittingly applied, is it surprising that the word stands for all that is courageous, noble, great, when used as a prefix in designating man or woman? In view of all that this one word pictures to our inner sight, can we wonder that we shrink appalled from the vicinity of one whom the words "disloyal," "traitor," rightly indicate? Ah, no, for *Loyal* is graven on the banner that covers multitudes of redeemed. It is graven on the foundation stones of a universe. The suns and stars flash it forth in glorious light as they move in their orbits, *true* to the hand that flung them into space.

Think you that any human being ever won and wore the honor of its bestowal, by a single act? Not so. It is woven as threads are woven in cloth of gold, into the essential fabric of the garment of the soul; and when that fabric is complete the soul need never ask itself a question as to whether it be right or wrong, when action is to be taken in any event, for "*It knows*"; It could not be false to Itself.

The dark places of the earth, the depths of the Eighth Sphere,[1] are fit habitations for the traitor, the disloyal.

---

[1] *Eighth Sphere* — a special channel or sphere connecting the Earth and Saturn, also known as the *Planet of Death*. It is designed to take care of the outflow of human masses that are not suitable for further evolution. These are the most vicious and hopelessly fallen people, as well as simply those who have not done any light-bearing deeds over the course of their numerous incarnations on the Earth. Their lower principles are decomposed into their primordial elements, which are absorbed by the corresponding elemental forces, while their higher principles will begin

The mental and moral effluvia which rises from the dead soul, the soul murdered by disloyalty, permits no one to be long deceived as to the nature of its simulacrum — the body — no matter how fair the body, how subtle the mind, to which that dead soul is attached.

If you cannot be true to the principles you have chosen to guide your lives, if you cannot be true to father or mother, wife or husband, nation or home; how can you be true to your own souls? How can you be true to your God — to your Higher Self?

If you find within yourself a lack of power to be loyal to all the duties that you have undertaken, begin now to spin the golden threads that you will need for that Christly fabric I have mentioned, by being true in little things; true to your obligations to your comrades; true to the trust placed in you, when you are left unwatched to sweep a floor or plow a field. The threads will broaden and strengthen and multiply, and one day you will all unexpectedly find there are enough to weave the fabric for the garment of the soul.

You cannot be true to yourself and false to your friend at the same time; the singing bird and the snake cannot live together in one field.

You cannot be true to God and false to your neighbor, for God and your neighbor are one.

"Truth" does indeed "lie at the bottom of a well," and you must look long and steadily if you would find it to star a diadem 'gainst your crowning. But falsehood ever lies close at hand, spreading a net for unwary feet, and, like all easy things — all illusions — murderous at its base.

Loyalty is the firstborn Son of Truth: disloyalty the bastard offspring of falsehood.

---

their process of evolution anew on Saturn, under the extremely difficult conditions of this two-dimensional world.

ASK EACH DAY

Thou who knowest that all life is ever ceaseless pulsing motion!

Thou who knowest that the sun must rise and set *each day*, and that every heartbeat is in perfect time and rhythm!

Thou who knowest that the food of yesterday will not sustain thy body for the morrow's toil!

Thinkest thou the cyclic law, immutable, will be repealed for thee, in that each day will bring thee nourishment for soul, unasked for and unsought by thee, or asked amiss?

Ah, no! A full supply of Christly bread awaits thine asking, but thou must ask *each day*, and ask in faith, or suffer in thy Soul as now thy body suffers from the lack of food when thou dost not provide.

LOOK WITHIN

Hath a miry slough opened 'neath thy straying feet and a storm cloud burst above thy head? Then hold thee still and look within.

There shalt thou find a place of refuge, a point of observation from which thou mayst sight the distant hills and the clear sky.

There, too, shalt thou find thy Guide and an open path.

THE NORTHERN WINDOWS

Open the Northern windows of thy soul, weak, unstable mortal.

Let in the bracing wind, the crystal genii of the ice, that they may rouse thee from the sodden sleep in which the Southern winds have bound thee. Long hast thou lain inert and pulseless 'neath the spell, powerless to strike a blow in thy defense. Thou canst not stand erect and wrestle with the Northern blasts, and so regain the strength and courage needful for thy battle with the hosts that throng the underworld.

Cast off the glamor. Bare thy breast to all the icy winds that sweep the Storm-King's realms. Though beaten to the earth again, and yet again, yet shall thou rise each time the stronger, and at length thou shalt be master of thyself, and therefore of thy fate.

DARKNESS

For eons now hath Evil stolen guise of darkness and dimmed thine inner eye, till it hath lost its power to pierce those shadowy depths, to find therein the rarest treasures life doth hold.

Thy little ones now enter life accursed with fear of darkness, as thou hast come accursed by thine own parent's fear, and so man doth perpetuate the curse from age to age. And yet, all peace, all rest, Death's brightest face, all germination and all growth — the holiest mysteries of life — are held within the folds of darkness.

When thou hast silenced all thy fears, and with thine ear attuned to her low murmurings, then shalt thou hear the softest melodies, the cradle songs, of the Great Mother as she sings her wearied children into sweetest sleep at setting of the day that they may gain the strength to greet the morrow's sun, and in her song will be revealed the mysteries of Night so long concealed.

MAKE ROOM FOR ME

Make room for me, while yet an hour remains before the Sands of Time have run their course in this dark Iron Age!

Make room, ye blind and sore of heart, ye who are smitten with the plagues of all the centuries past! Make room, ye heedless revelers in transitory Pleasure Halls! Make room all ye who fail to see the writing on the wall, who read no message in the stars whose cyclic sweeps are marking plain the coming of my day!

A little hour is left thee to tear down the bars 'twixt thee and me, my child; to widen out the spaces in thine heart and make room, ere falls the day I come with Scales of Justice in my hands.

I, who cry to thee must leave the wand of mercy far behind when weighted with the heavy scales I bear, and in that day the choice will be no longer thine or mine, but His who sends me and who rules alike o'er ah.

THE SHADOW

BE PATIENT with the shadows — thou climber of the heights — not only with thine own but with the shadows of all others.

Remember, thou seest only shadows with thy deceptive sense of sight; the real man, the real woman is hidden from thy view.

Only with thy soul sight canst thou glimpse beyond the haunting shadowy caricature of thy true Self — that caricature which, like unto automata, may sing and dance or sob and cry according to the will controlling it, the hand which holds the string.

So be patient with thy shadow for, when its little day is ended, its purpose all fulfilled, it will disappear, and in its place thou wilt behold the Self — that Self which, since the dawn of thy creation, has been standing back in the Silence of Eternity, watching the antics of its shadows and "pulling the strings."

ANSWER ME

I LED thee to the gate, and fain would keep thy hand and lead thee on till thou hadst reached the Central Flame, and entered in, and all thy dross were purged away. Then couldst thou stand alone, freed from Maya's curse, in likeness unto Me.

I pray thee tell Me, was the gate too small for thy bent back or did the Flames affright thee so thou couldst not see the glory just beyond? Or did the demons of the underworld lay hold on thee and drag thee back and loose thy hold on Me?

Canst thou make answer truthfully when thou with Me hast entered the Great Silence? For so, mayhap, the path may open once again, and thou be stronger grown.

For know thee well, thou, who art Mine own, thou canst not reach the Temple Gate save with My hand in thine, for we are one.

ENDURANCE

IN YOUR last extremity, when heedless of all else save the ever deepening, despairing cry of your soul then being smothered on your drawn lips; when your whole being seems submerged in one intense longing for surcease from the anguish of the fitful fever that has consumed your courage, your will, your desires — then I bid you strive to reach out and hold on to the jutting rock on the bank of life's stream, the rock we name Endurance — the rock which rises above and beyond all others on those banks, and upon which is graven the message: "However hard, however distasteful and exacting the temporalities of the day, with the dawn of a new day, a change will come as surely as that new sun has gilded the East. However dark and swirling the waters of that Life Stream may be, at the close of the day of your despair, there must come another day, when the whispered 'Peace, be still!' will quiet the waves and so permit you to swim safely and peacefully into the haven of your hopes, if you have hold of that one *Invincible Rock.*"

THE SCOFFER

HAST thou chosen then? Thou pitiful scoffer at Holy Things! Chosen in Pride and Ignorance, only to awaken one day to sorrow unspeakable!

The earth rises to greet the falling sun when its day is done, even as the Soul rises to greet its descending God when its little day is done. Night cometh; the night when no man may work; and thou, like unto a bird, must needs seek a resting place; but unlike the bird, which seeks wisely and well the topmost branches of its chosen tree, thou, the fruit of all past ages, thou, built in the image of a God, taught by the Devas of the higher spheres, thou buildest thy resting place on the shifting sands of life's most fitful Ocean; the sands which that Ocean in its wrath will surely overflow, and whose outgoing tide will bear thee swiftly downward, outward to extinction. None can give thee help for thou hast despised the rocks to which thy kind hath clung since Time began for man.

Thou hast closed thine ears to the voice of thy heart.

Thou hast made of the Gods a mock and of their messenger a butt.

Thou hast chosen thy lot when thine was the choice and must abide therein.

Thou hast bartered thy birthright for a bauble and the bauble is broken.

THE STRICKEN SOUL

Right joyfully doth all the heavenly host give welcome unto him who strikes the load of evil from an overburdened soul, to save that soul alive; for he who hath been worsted in the fight with all the powers of darkness hath never strength to free himself unaided.

And he who lifts the burden from a stricken soul by sacrifice of self, will find the virtues of the Diamond Soul concealed therein.

Right royally doth Hell's low minions welcome him who casts the mirrored image of his own foul nature o'er the one, who, trusting in the vaunted honor, purity, and power of him he called by all the sacred names man gives to friend, hath placed no shield before his naked soul, for such a demon in the guise of man doth lead the van in those foul depths where devils congregate.

LET GO

Let go! Let go, ye fearful, cowering souls! Let go the form, half God, half fiend, which primitive and mindless man made in his own crude image, and other men less crude have foisted on a throne, and forced their fellow men to worship!

If thou wouldst picture God unto thyself — limit the eternally limitless ere thine own soul can rest and understand — then picture to thyself an image far transcending human love and wisdom, power and justice, nor be content with less. A God so pure that no created thing could sully it, so clean that every unclean thought of man must die aborning ere it reached Its Presence. A God who could not build a Hell for human kind till all the nascent fires had first consumed His own diviner essence, and from the residue thereof create the great Redeemer of mankind, One, Inseparable — purifying by His touch the vilest thing created.

Only such a God is worthy of the reverence of the Sons of God.

Let go of other Gods, and seek thy God according to thy strength and power of search.

IT

MAYHAP you name It Sacrifice, or Joy, or All fulfillment. Perchance you picture It in mind as that which lights the Sun, or as the law which holds intact the whirling stars in space. Or you may clothe It in a garment pure, enfolding man and maid, when sound of wedding bell falls on the ear.

What'er the name bestowed, what form the thought has taken, or the fancy subtly wrought, It always bears the sign and visage of the Godhead, that *radiant energy, creator and preserver*, which man has designated *Love*. Love the leveler; the all-pervading principle of Life; the Light that lighteth every man.

The wielder of all power in heaven and earth. The Unifier wise and strong, which joins all worlds, all systems, sky and earth, the rootlets of the tiniest blade of grass, the hearts of men, in one eternal bond.

Love washes out all bitterness, all fear and hate, and makes a place of peace where once was only strife. It streams from every mother's eyes and fires the pride in every father's heart.

It downward turns the sordid side of toil and brings to light the side of recompense.

A mystery of mysteries. A worker of life's miracles is Love, the purest and most precious jewel in God's treasure house.

THE THREEFOLD WARNING

ONCE at the breaking of his vow; twice, if under exceptionally great pressure the soul yields; thrice it may be in a last vital extremity — may a warning note be struck from the seats of the Mighty, to fall on the ears of the Twice-begotten — the Neophyte — thenceforward, the stillness of the Great Silences.

The glamor cast by the Jinn of the underworld, over a betrayer of his trust, will drift away like the mist before the sun, when the light from the torch of seminal Truth, held in the hand of the Mighty, is turned upon it. Naught but glamor could turn the heart of the Twice-born from the seat of power, and send him adrift.

"Great is glamor!" — "Great is the King!" cry the hapless victims of its power, until the light of Truth is turned thereon.

THE PEACE OF GOD

GATHER up in one bouquet as thou wouldst gather roses rare, the loves of all the creatures of all worlds, of man, of animal, of plant, of whirling planet, sun and nebulae — the loves that rise as perfumes to the skies. Add to these all shades, and combinations of all shades that Light hath flashed to color. Then bind them with the force of every note and tone which ever gushed from throat of man, and bird, and beast, in song and praise — the chords of that sweet song, the morning stars have sung since dawn of life, the rustle of the winds, the moanings of the waves; and if thou hast no name for such a marvel, thou mayest call it God. Then, if thou canst see and know the spirit of those loves, those rays of color, perfumes, notes, and chords, and feel it fold thee close when one short day of time is closed, as, at the setting of the sun, the mother folds her little one and hushes it to sleep and only lays herself to rest when the great Bird of Life hath folded close its wings, then and only then, shalt thou — the offspring of that God — feel and know the *peace* of God.

THE TEMPLE PLAN

NO MAN, no host of men, laid hand upon or wrought God's Temple plan, nor can a man or host of men destroy or mar that plan.

High in the heavens unfurled it hangs for eyes unclouded, clarified of self, to see.

Blest indeed is he, who seeing, builds upon the screen of mind a replica of that great plan which is eternal in the soul of time.

Thrice blest is he who lays a stone upon the breast of earth and lays so true to line that other hands may build upon it, that other men may lay their all upon it, and so may raise a simulacrum of that first, most wondrous plan of all, each precious gem of which, cemented by the sacrificial blood shed drop by drop from human hearts will last for aye. A Temple made by human hands indeed shall man yet build; a Temple worthy of the presence and the peace of God.

THE GRAVE OF SIN

CAREFULLY, tenderly, bury thou the faults of thy brethren, for in their graves will lie the embryonic forms which later will rise regenerated as virtues.

If thou refusest burial, and leavest them at large to gather substance from the vile corroding thoughts of those who think to kill, then wilt thou become in part the slayer of thy brethren.

On the grave of dead sins may rise the soul purified, and if thou hast helped to dig the grave which held those sins, then shalt thou be partaker in the resurrection of that soul.

YE TOO

"WILL ye, too, leave me, best beloved of all?" So cries the Christ as in the garden of Gethsemane — the world — again he stands unarmed, unterrified, yet lonely with a loneliness no child of Earth can understand.

"Will ye, too, leave me, ye whom I have loved with love surpassing that of earthly kin?"

"Will ye too leave me to the wrath of foes, the tiger claws of human passion, the sneers, contempt, betrayal of the mob which in its ignorance hath yielded to the demon Hate which now would lay me low?"

"Will ye too leave me, ye whom in your infancy I fed and healed and saved from foes unnumbered?" "Will ye too leave me, going where mine enemies have gone, to raise a cross that I may die upon for loving ye too well?"

OPPORTUNITY

GOLDEN opportunity comes once to every man, twice to a selfless man, but never thrice to the same man in the same life-cycle.

Happy is he who hath seized the first; twice blest is he who reaps the reward of his first in his second; despair alone is the portion of him who idly awaits the coming of a third.

The two-leaved door of life's mysteries will shut close on the last, and will no more open for him until they fly back to let his purged soul through at the beginning of a new life-cycle.

THE DIAMOND SOUL

WHAT boots it, the pain, the longing, the weariness of the moment — the single moment out of the Eternities — to him who sees each trial as a gage of the great battle he is fighting for the crown of self-recognition, and who knows that with every conquest a *white stone* is added to the Crown of the Diamond Soul.

The moment with its burden will pass, but the Diamond Soul will hail the dawn of every new age, 'till Time is lost in Eternity.

THE RICH

Of all the poverty bestead, this brutal age doth hold in clanking chain — the naked savage in the winter's storm — the skulking outcast in the city's street — none are so poor, none so want-betrayed as he who lays his all upon some self-made game, and *winning*, *loses* his own soul.

Of all the rich, the powerful of earth — the monarch on his throne; the holder of a thousand slaves, of lands, of mines, and golden store untold — none are so rich, so measurelessly rich in all that constitutes true wealth, as he who knows and loves his fellow man so well, the treasure chest of God's great love hath opened unto him.

BIRDS OF PREY

Ho, ye servitors of the Thrice-born, ye jinns of the underworld! By the power with which ye are invested, by the mission with which ye are intrusted, go ye to the betrayers of our trust, the foresworn traitors of the battle's eve, the forked tongued of the dark star-earth, and blind ye their eyes that they may not see the glory; hold ye their ears that they may not hear the call of the blessed.

Birds of prey are they that have befouled their own nests, outraged the mother who bore them, and uncovered the nakedness of the father who gave them form. What place is there for such as these in the new age and among the true-hearted?

So, do ye to them as ye are bidden. Blind their eyes and deafen their ears, lest they see and hear that which they have not earned, and that which is forfeit to them; lest they take the bread of life from between the lips of the worthy, and give it unto the dogs of war and confusion.

SORROW

Let sorrow do its perfect work in thee, my child, that so it raise thee to the heights where dwell the Gods. Failing this, take care lest from the dark recesses of thine own sick mind thou bringest forth the poison seething there and spew it out of thy mouth, to infect the weak.

When sorrow does not cleanse and purify the heart, it sinks into some dark recess therein, inflames and suppurates, then reinfects both heart and mind. A victim of such foul disease becomes as doth the leper, a source of dread and danger to all who cross his path. He casts reflections from his sin-sick soul on those who in compassion would minister to him, and sees his own depraved, erupted likeness in their faces, as he would see it in a mirror. He knows not love nor pity, mercy nor forgiveness, and only lives to blast or kill, rebellious to the last.

Then truly, sin and sorrow are but two opposing poles of one of life's deep mysteries. The victim of the one may fall and sink e'en to the lowest level, or he may rise to the greatest heights attained to by the other.

THE HIGHWAY

Lo! I stand and cry for help to build the highway over which myriad footsteps may pass — the footsteps of the hosts so long oppressed, the little ones now trodden underfoot of man.

Even while my cry rings forth thou turnest far away thy gaze upon some short and narrow trail, and sit thee down to wait another call — or sayest to thyself, "the highway he would build would be too wide, and far too long for me to tread, the paving stones not such as I would choose." "He plans no shade on either side, no mound where I might sit me down to rest. If I could choose the workmen, lay the pavement, fix the compensation for the toil, and build a gate at either end to bar mine enemy — then would I answer, and give myself in service true."

Alas, that while thou heedest not my cry, my little ones — thy little ones — the poor, the halt and blind are stumbling, falling back, or being thrown by press of those behind.

No highway has been made for them, or thee; nor can it be without thy help.

TRUTH

WOULDST thou know the Truth — the pure, the undefiled — the sacred Truth, by means of which man is made free and strong?

Wouldst thou know the Truth, thou shrinking, stricken, smitten victim of thine own untruth, thou blind, and lame, and halt of body or of soul, who pleads for mercy to the powers thou hast defied?

Wouldst thou *now* know the Truth? Then bend thine ear to me.

Like calls to like throughout the bounds of Time and space. From ameba to man, and thence to angel host the call rings strong and clear, and ever doth the answer come in kind; then, how couldst thou behold and know the Truth if lips of thine are dank with falsehood, if lure of mind and body doth beguile thy fellow man to his undoing, if foul deceit and treachery to friend and foe alike hath cast deep shadows o'er thy path of life and hid the face of Truth from thee?

Wouldst thou *now* know the Truth? *Then think and speak the Truth* so far as now thou knowest it and Truth herself, unclothed, in all her fullness, beauty, strength, will come to dwell with thee. Unabashed, thine eyes shall seek her face, and seeking there shalt find "the Peace that passeth understanding," the key to all the mysteries of life.

FROM GOD TO MAN

I SENT thee forth alone, unbound, in the morning of thy life, into a wide, wide world wherein no foot of man had strayed. I sent thee forth with the heart of a child, and a clean white mind wherein was writ no record of sin or shame, or prophecy of pain.

I gave thee the Stars for thy toys, and the Sky for a place to play; and I bade thee grow 'till thy head o'er-topped the highest arch of Heaven.

I only bade thee bring to me at the close of thy Day of Time a *pure man's heart* and a *childlike mind* in return for *my trust in thee*.

THE HEART OF GOD

THOU homeless wanderer in trackless wastes, knowest thou not that the door in the garden of thy heart opens into the garden of the Heart of God, where the flowers of Love, Wisdom, and Power bud, blossom and bear fruit for thy plucking? Open that door and enter into thine own divinity.

The Heart of God is the container of the divine in all things and creatures, and therefore of the divine in thee.

Only within that Heart canst thou find thy true self, and all things that are thine own.

HOLD HIGH THY TRUST

FAR more doth it injure thee than it doth thy friend when thou hurlest a poison tipped shaft of suspicion at him.

A pure white page of thine own book of life is splashed with the black ooze of the Eighth Sphere if such a shaft from thy hand doth hit thy friend. The stain of that ooze is indelible. Little by little it would seep through every succeeding page of that book upon which the name of thy friend was writ and one day thou wouldst find thou hadst lost thy friend — thy most priceless possession.

Then, hold high thy trust. Far better is it that thou sufferest injury through thy trust, if needs be, than that thou shouldst betray thy friend, even to thine own heart.

THY GOLDEN OPPORTUNITY

Cast the sunlight of the Self obliquely on the cares of daily life, and they will swiftly turn to golden opportunities, e'en as now doth Dangma's[1] beams, at close of day, glorify the bubbles on the ocean's waves.

The bubbles break, their glory vanishes, but memory of their beauty clings about and satisfies the heart, when life is sad.

Even so the cares will pass, but opportunities for love and service pure remain to raise the frailest of the sons of man to stature of the Gods.

GROW WINGS AND FLY HIGH

Row wings, my child, wings of pure thought, aspiration and high courage; wings strong and virile enough to bear thee to the heights of life, where safe placed thou mayest glimpse the pit now hidden from thy view by murky clouds.

The wind from the heights, fanned into motion by thy wings, will blow away the ashes from its mouth and give thee sight of lurid flames and hosts of demons spawned by Hatred, Greed and Avarice of man. Full of guile are they and wise enough to seek and find the entrance to the soul which gave them birth for food and nourishment on which to grow 'til strong enough to drive that soul from its own place and take possession full.

Then grow wings, my child, and fly high; there is naught between thee and the stars but thine own will.

---

[1] *Dangma* (*Sanskrit*, "purified soul") — a Seer and an Initiate; one who has attained full wisdom.

THE WORD ETERNAL

O MAN of many words, who knoweth not *The Word* thy noise doth hide from thee; thou reveler within and squanderer of God's most precious gift; thou who feeleth no regret for wasted lesser lives, and in thy mad extravagance doth often drench the sphere with which thou art encompassed with streams of energy so wide, so powerful for good or ill, that thou wouldst stand abashed but for thy ignorance, thy foolish exaltation of the *shadow* to the throne of Wisdom, thereby rendering thee a piteous object of compassion in the eyes of those — thine Elder Brothers — who stand and wait beside the inner gate. They will not enter lest mankind be left alone, a guideless, oarless vessel on the shoreless ocean of eternal life. The gate which they have won the right to open as they will, and pass to endless bliss and union with the God they have long sought.

But, ah, how little understood by man, this sacrifice divine! How oft doth puny man fling back into their faces all the gifts laid on the sacrificial fires, and cry, "I will have none of thee, thou God or Christ, or manikin, whate'er thou art! I will choose and go my way without thy guidance or the aid of those who worship such as Thou." Alas, he knows not that long ere now he had sunk to nothingness were it not for those he now contemns. He knows not that he holds within his feeble clasp the instrument to sound the key to all the greater mysteries now in suspension held within that shoreless ocean; the key which sets the bounds or breaks them, to all forms, all lesser lives. But if that key is sounded, he must yield his lower life in rite of sacrifice; that fife of sense to which he clings tenaciously, beside which other forms of life seem cold and dead.

He cannot see as yet that in thus yielding he will find himself, the Self he long since lost.

Only he who *gives his life* shall find and keep his life eternally.

NEW BIRTHS

DIVINE Love — Life — Law, brings to new birth and opportunity each gladsome new spring, new life for all the myriad lesser lives created through past cycles. It clothes them with new garments bright and beautiful, and says to each in turn with tender touches warm and moist, "Take thou the gifts I bring to thee and use them for thy glory and thy growth."

Of all the countless hordes of living things which love creates, man alone dare fling those gifts disdainfully aside and say unto the giver, "I will not grant myself, nor yet my fellowman, the glory of new births — the springtimes of recurring cycles; for only age and death await my kind when youth is past"; and saying so he binds his soul in bonds he will not break, and wearily plods on to pain and dissolution, blind to the lessons Love hath showered on him, heedless to the end.

WILL DIVINE

IF THOU wouldst waken from thy sleep of ignorance and sloth to knowledge of the destiny decreed for him who yields obedience in the faith, then make of thine own self a channel wide and straight that so the Will of God — a living stream — may flow direct, unchallenged on its course. All the refuse of thy many lives that stream will bear away to be transmuted to its depths, and on its breast will float thy new-cleansed bark of life, its pure white sails unfurled to all the world. Manned by courage, decked with Purpose, anchored by a Will set in a prow of Wisdom, who or what could change the course of such a bark save God and thee?

SEEK THE CAUSE

IF THOU wouldst seek the primal cause of thine unfaith in God or man or thing, and seek that cause with all thy soul unmindful of the heights or depths where it now lies, determined only to accept the truth when found, regardless of the wound to self that knowledge may inflict — then seek within thine heart for time and place and purpose when thou didst injure, grieve or wound the God, the man, the thing wherein thy faith now lieth dead. For as the arrow flieth straight toward a mark, so flies the cause of wrongful deed or thought straight to the mark of its effect — thy present faithlessness.

It may be but a seed of thought or word by which the wound was made, but being sown and watered by the stream of circumstances, its growth and blossoming, its fruit and seeding, are as sure as darkness after light.

Faith is a tender plant. It will not bear the storms of Hate, Suspicion or Neglect. Its very tenderness is of the Love and tenderness of God.

THE VEIL

SWIFTLY turn thy face toward me, my child. Be thou not content with any shade or fleeting form made in my likeness. I have fixed my face within thine heart. See to it that thou tear away the veils the Fates[1] by thee have woven 'twixt that face and thee, e'en though thine heart should bleed afresh with every outdrawn thread.

When there be naught 'twixt thee and Me, then shalt thou know My glory and My power for thine.

Seek thou Me, my child, and not another in my guise, for I have chosen thee and thou art Mine.

From out the figments of the mind, from threads spun from the woof of reason and the warp of lower will, man weaves veil after veil between himself and God. He names them Intellect and Purpose, Self-assertion, Independent-action, and never knows that Love and Wisdom in their parturition pains are crying out for birth within his heart 'till sore beset, choking, strangling, panting in their folds, he strips away each veil and frees his prisoned heart.

Then alone doth he behold his Father's Face.

---

[1] *Fates* — the goddesses of destiny, usually represented as three sisters.

THE PERFECT ONE

WHEN every unit of mankind can vision to itself the same ideal of That which now each one doth form in separate guise and name the "Perfect One," then will Humanity approach its long sought goal. Perfection to the mind of one is imperfection to the minds of others, and many Gods of many minds will never satisfy for long the soul which sprang full grown from One.

"The Perfect One" yet stands alone, serene, supreme, awaiting the glad day when man *en masse*[1] shall see his beauty, holiness and power, and seeing, shall stretch forth its myriad arms and cry, "Enough! Now have we seen the end of all travail. Now have we found ourselves, in Thee — The One Eternal Self."

THE COMMON CHORD

WHEN Father — Mother — Son, the Triune God is once more seated on the long vacated throne within the human heart, to rule again that heart in majesty and love, then man will rise to sovereignty o'er all the lesser lives which now obstruct the path to power.

Man may hot tear apart the common Chord of C — the Chord of Life, and Love, and Law, to strike a single tone of that vast Trinity alone, without sustaining loss immeasurable. For in the spaces left between, the minor tones will silent lie — those tones which wake "the Angels of the Voice" to guard the path to Power.

THE LIGHT WITHIN

THOU who art as a star to some unselfish, tender heart which beats alone for thee, how great thy task, how sore thy punishment if thou dost fail to sense within thyself that which first, called forth adoring love within the heart which set thee high above all else on earth.

---

[1] *En masse (French)* — as a whole; all together as a group.

He who saith that love is blind doth utter a foul travesty on truth, for love is keen of vision, and love hath seen a ray of the divine in thee behind the darkened windows of thy soul, though it be all unseen by other eyes than love's.

Deep calls to deep alway. Divinity doth seek Divinity where e'er it may be found. And if some other soul hath sought and found a ray of the Divine in thee, how humble shouldst thou be, how thankful that there yet is time to cleanse those darkened windows that the light within may seek its source and in its passing reach and bless the one who first uncovered it and brighten all the world for thee and thine.

THE WEB

Wrapped in Illusion's web thou liest now bereft of power to tear that web apart and glimpse the Real — the Christ — the Only Son, the First Begotten of the One Unmanifest — the One in whom all Truth, all Joy, all fruit of Sorrow borne in patience and submission, hath met and blended in the Kalpas past, and still must meet in Kalpas yet to come — the One who stands supreme and dauntless in the midst of that Illusion thou hast deemed thyself. There is but One. The countless suns in space could hold no Second, Third or Fourth.

When Truth unveils herself all error, pain and longing vanish as doth the dew before the morning sun. When man is more than man he stands revealed as
Christ to those who having eyes may see. Yet other men in ignorance still stone the man, unseeing Christ.

DEATH

From the conception and the travail of the Gods is born the soul of man. Then shall the fragments of that soul be scattered as the dust of earth when once the power that sent it forth is inward turned to other spheres.

Ah, ye who fear that Death may follow on the *closing* of the last short chapter of the book of life that thou shalt read with mortal eyes; ye knoweth naught of life in essence or its power to search into the fields of space — the utmost reaches of the inner spheres — to clothe itself in garb more subtle, tenuous and lasting, than is the coarse, unbeautiful and transient raiment worn by it in mortal guise.

As clothes the soul of rose or violet in garb of sweetest perfume as its body withers, dies, so clothes the soul of man in sweeter perfume still, arising from the kindly deed, the sacrifice, unselfish service for mankind, when wearied, worn with toil and torn with pain, at length it leaves its mortal form to mingle with the dust from which it sprang.

FEAR

IF YOU misuse the divine afflatus of genius by prostituting it for your own selfish use or pleasure you will be consumed in its fires. It belongs to the whole universe, and when in your pitiable self-conceit you would attempt to make of it a reflector of your own egotistic personality, it draws you into its flames and consumes you utterly.

To you as well as to every human being there will someday stalk a live fiend of fear quivering with uncertainty, and always thereafter it will walk by your side. You may sometimes close your eyes to its grinning face and lull yourself into a feeling of security for a little while, but deep down in your soul you will know it is always there; waiting for you to open your eyes to its presence again; waiting for some sign of physical or mental weakness that will render you less capable of self-protection, in order to spring forward, leer into your face and say, "You are my slave."

Full enlightenment will never come to mortal man while he is treading the path outlined by all the milestones he has set and marked with the blood shed by his victims.

Only as he enters that path will satisfaction come to him. Only as he leaves that path may he behold the radiant light of the sun of righteousness which alone can vanquish the demons of fear.

Knowing this, prepare to win endurance and power to walk in darkness, unafraid.

THE UNFINISHED

If you but knew the little seed you set today, mayhap in carelessness, in pride or subtlety, would grow on through the coming years, mature and bear its fruit for you to eat in sorrow on another day; if you but knew the tale which you commenced to tell today, the task which you began, would not be finished until all their consequences faced you in your hour of test and proved to be the drops which ran the measure of your trial over on the farther side, would you not leave the seed unplanted, the tale untold? Would you not hold your hand from execution?

Remember, fulfillment ever cometh otherwise. No act or word is finished on the day it was begun or spoken. No man hath ever lived so long that he completed any task begun; and "on the path" the unfinished parts of every thought, word and deed, in all their latent grace, their crudeness or their loathsomeness, will start up unexpectedly to help or hinder as the case may be.

Then would it not be well to carefully consider seed or word or act ere it hath passed forever from thy keeping?

THE RIGHT TO SEEK

Wouldst thou seek the King of the dazzling face, the Master of men and things? Then take from thy back the heavy load that bends thy face to the ground. Free the viscid mud from thy bleeding feet; change thy rotten staff for a conqueror's sword. Smother the moan that comes to thy lips; change the cry of pain to a pecan of praise.

Lift up thy head; fix thine eyes on the sun and fight for the right to seek. The right to seek on the selfsame path that the Godmen of old have walked; the right to die without shame of men as the ancient heroes died: The coward who feareth death or fife can never walk that path. Its thorns and briers, its sharpened rocks, pierce heart and feet alike.

If thou wouldst seek aright and find the object of thy search, that glorious King of the dazzling face, then fight for the right to seek.

EMOTION

There comes an hour in the life of every awakened disciple when the cold, merciless scalpel of mind searches each emotion, each feeling, to its center of being and forces the Self, which stands between the mentality and the senses, into the position of judge and executioner combined.

In seeming cruelty it cuts away every vestige of the comfortable, comforting, excuse-provoking wrappings which have bound the Self, and leave that Self naked and inconceivably desolate for the time being; yet it is only in such hours that the great destiny, the purpose of being, is revealed to the individual Self.

Not that there is necessarily an underestimation of the divine purpose in the creation of the emotions as a result of such revelation, but that they may be rightly placed and thenceforth rightly used, instead of being permitted to rule where they should only serve, as is generally the case with undeveloped man.

When acute feeling overwhelms the sense of righteousness and justice in a given instance, wrong is inevitably the result. If the emotions, the feelings, can be used to counteract the harsher acts of the retribution which justice demands, thus preventing justice from descending to cruelty and injustice, they are then in their right provinces and put to right uses.

THY CHOICE

On one side, the bare mountain, windswept, sun-beaten, stripped of all verdure, desolate to the human eye, wearisome to the muscle-tortured limbs of the climber, straining his panting heart till it bursts its sheath and pours forth its contents in a living stream over the torn and tortured feet which are bearing it upward.

On the other side, the deeply wooded valley with its trickling streams, its moss covered banks, its tender clinging vines and ravishingly beautiful flowers. A valley wherein the tired, footsore pilgrim may lay him down to rest, and with his eyes fixed lingeringly on the quivering leaves, the soft shadows thrown by the tender glances of a summer sun, sink into oblivion, forgetful of all the past, careless of all that the future may bring to him.

Ah, 'tis a strong, brave and unselfish soul that can withstand the charms of the valley, and deliberately choose the bare mountain side, while yet unknowing what the beating winds are bearing to him from other, inner worlds; while yet unconscious of the hidden life and glory in that unshaded sun, unseeing the great Angel of the Gates who, poised upon the mountaintop, awaits his last faint footfall.

If one might know; if one might see or even dream of the final results of his unaided, toilsome journey up through the mountain side and through the world of shadows, then 'twere easy to make choice between the paths. Then all pain would pleasure be, and every bare, drear stretch of desert or of mountain side within his soul would blossom as the rose and lily bloom in sunny places in his earthly garden.

But in the dark, when not a ray of light from the great sun of life is shed to point to danger or to nearing death; when facing him or at his own right hand are all the delights and joys of life, and soft, melodious voices plead with him to give his soul to pleasure and to ease. And on the other side is Silence, vast, unbroken Silence, save when moan or cry of pain falls on his straining ear from one hard pressed; one who travels that same way; one whose lips are crushed into the earth on which he lies, to still their trembling and force back the cry so near escaping them, the cry that would rob him of strength to rise again and press still farther on.

Ah, this would try the mettle of the bravest soul, and yet, My Child, thou must make thy choice and make it for all Time and Eternity, when thou art called to choose. Then would it not be well for thee that thou shouldst even now prepare thyself for choice by seeking for the hidden things within thine heart, these things which lie beneath the outer seemings of thy daily life, thy stolen joys, thy pains and sacrifices; instead of waiting for the day when, unprepared for it, the call shall come to thee and thou shalt find thou hast no wisdom for the choice, no strength to follow where thy soul would lead if lead it might, because the power of choosing rightly had long been buried in thy pleasure seeking, or in thy pride, thine avarice or thine ambition.

Mark well my words; they will occur to thee again and yet again in the days to come. Thou hast demanded power of choice, demanded it in aspiration, prayer and act, and near at hand that choice lies now to thee.

LOVE'S OFFICES

IT IS NOT by the love it inspires that the individual soul attains to bliss and satisfaction, but by the love it gives unselfishly, seeking no return. Love undesired, unasked, is worthless in the eyes of the beloved and feeds on the heart it dwells within.

God — Divine Love — desires and asks for human love, therefore prizes that love and pours forth Divine love on all creatures, thus satisfying his own heart.

A woman may hate and betray one of her own sex to gain the love of man, while man despises and betrays the woman for love of ambition; thus the law of compensation strives to strike a balance when Love is degraded in unworthy shrines.

The cruse of the bereft — the widowed heart, is filled with wine and oil of life — Divine Love — as often as its contents are emptied. Widowed by loss of human love once lain in the grave of earthly desire, that heart is filled to overflowing with Divine Love.

THE WORLD PAIN

THE pain of the world beats hard on the heart athrob with sympathy. The answer to the "why" of that pain comes home to the "open-eyed" with every recurring stroke like unto the stroke of the hammer as it falls on the anvil. The gnawing demons of ignorance, vice and greed first stupefy the mind, then throttle and crush the body back into the soil whence it came, to refertilize that soil for another crop — another race of men.

Again the birth pang, again the childhood, middle life and age, a repetition of the same old story. Always the world pain beats on the tender heart; always the eternal "why?" — the protest against suffering. Always the strangling, stifling rebellion against the impotence, the powerlessness of man to compel his brother man to seek the God who is ever close at hand, ever waiting for the beast in man to die and the angel to be born.

"*Cui bono?*"[1] cry the careless, the indifferent; "let us dance and sing and leave the pain to those who love it." "How long, O Lord, how long?" moan the martyr and the saint, "how long ere cometh Thy salvation?"

"More, more, give me more," screams the wastrel, the libertine, in the depths of his stag-like passion or drunken frenzy; "more, more," always, "more."

From on high, the Christ on the Cross where man has hung Him, on which He suffers, from which at times He smiles, wafts down into the aching, sympathetic heart the incense of patient waiting, a breath of the peace ever flowing from the soul of pain, and that heart grows still. And once again the Christ smiles.

---

[1] *Cui bono* (Latin) — "for whose benefit?" or "for what purpose?"

THE NEXT STEP

Have you been stalled on that last step you took? Are you now looking into the gulf of despair? Does your sinking heart refuse you energy for another push? Are your eyes blinded to everything save the bottomless pit into which you have cast the hopes of your young manhood, the finely wrought fabric of your girlish dreams? Have you marked the hideous word, "failure," on your life screen, believing the end of all things has come for you?

Then, force that heavy heart to another upward push; raise your eyes to the step which is just faintly appearing on the horizon of your mind and then *raise your foot*, and lol before you can realize it that next step has been taken and you are on a wide stretch of new country, the gulfs and pits have disappeared, hopes and dreams are in process of realization, a new day has dawned, a new lease of life entered upon.

Have you thought of the other men, the other women — those men and women whom you now look up to with unbridled admiration, but whose hearts failed them as yours has failed you — have you thought of those who sank in utter helplessness and weariness upon the stones which covered the last tread they had gained, when they thought of the heights yet to climb ere they could reach their goal and which overwhelmed and cast them into the gulf of despair? Would you know how these men and women climbed out of that gulf; how they conquered the demons who would have pushed them into the pit?

There was only one way for them, as there is only one way for you to accomplish that great feat. It is a very simple way; *just raise your eyes to the sun* and *push on* to the *next step*. Do not weary your heart and brain by thinking of the heights or the depths; think only of the *one short step* which when gained may be the "open sesame" to a greater height.

Bind the word *Persistence* over your forehead, and the word *Endurance* over your heart, and not all the demons in Hades nor all your enemies on earth can prevent the final attainment of your ideal.

It is always "the next step" of life's ladder that daunts you when with faltering limbs and wearied brain you have reached the halfway tread; not the thought of the perils behind or far ahead of you.

THE OBSTRUCTION

HE WHO fails to perceive the *nature* of the obstruction which dams up the mouth of any stream of his life will uselessly waste all effort to remove the obstruction, and only give the elementary forces of nature more power to increase its dimensions.

If the huge logs of a denuded forest are set free on the bosom of a stream, turning its currents and blocking its mouth, the wise man will not lose time in using a tool with which he would remove a sandbar from the same stream. He will use the tool made for such a purpose.

The fool saith in his heart, I will build a still higher obstruction on the crest of the lesser and so revenge myself upon the stream. He takes no thought of the nature of the waters which swiftly and silently will undermine his structure and carry both his work and himself out to the ocean into which they empty.

THE NINE STEPS

GOD, Nature, Law (call it what you will), the same beneficent, all-powerful energy that evolves a God from a stone, decrees that the spiritual eyes of the self-born shall be blinded for nine cycles, owing to Ills desire for liberty, as the material eyes of lower animals are blinded for nine days after birth by the pre-natal influence of the mother, and so decrees in order to restrict overweening desire for full liberty of action, which is one of the first desires to manifest in the animal as well as in man.

As the young animal is mercifully blinded to protect itself from material dangers, so man is blinded to the possible dangers that confront him on the path he is climbing, until a fixed measure of the power of endurance is won during each of the minor cycles — nine steps, which lead to the mountaintop — the greatest height of attainment for him.

If he should look down into the depths from some midway step, he would become so confused, so dizzy and powerless, that he could not save himself. So the Great Law blinds him to the sheer fall from the mountaintop, until he has reached the highest point and won the power to look unabashed and indifferently down and over the path he has come.

The eyes of the Diamond Soul must fall equally upon the Light from above and upon the shadow cast by the bitumen which lines that path.

THE STREAM OF SACRIFICE

Only he who hath eyes to behold and a heart to feel hath power to see beneath the surface of the stream of sacrifice which gushes from the open gate of the seven worlds and gathers volume and momentum with every moan of pain and sorrow wrung from human lips. That stream whose source is in the heart of God and which flows into the ocean of Infinity.

The crest of each smiling wave is dotted with the bruised leaves of the Tree of Life; each leaf of that tree of life to crush in the maw of the great Wheel of Time, until there is no longer semblance of form and only its aroma remains to sweeten the fields of Space.

But who can sound its depths or bring therefrom the treasures wrought by every sacrificial rite — to be the marriage portion of the Soul for whom the bridegroom waits — the Christ who knows the end from the beginning and sees his blood-stained face on every bruised and broken leaf? He claims His own when Time, the great illusion, is no more.

THE NEED OF PAIN

Wouldst thou banish pain and sorrow from thy life, ne'er to feel again the stab, the crunch, the grind of tender flesh, the sick despair of soul when sorrow's clutch lays hold?

Wouldst thou resign the right to feel the tender beat of angel's wings when Pain hath done its perfect work?

Then know that with its passing from thy field of life, if driven thence by desire and will, goes all thy fitness for release.

Every line upon thy face or heart, the graving stylus of thy sorrow and thy pain hath limned thereon, hath marked the lintel of an open door through which thou hast the power to pass to freedom if thou wilt — freedom from the dungeons which thou hast dug by means of broken law.

THE STONES OF SACRIFICE

As thy forbears of another race and age did bear their aged and weak and sore beset up to the mountaintop and fling them to the stones beneath to perish, so now thou bearest others of thy forbears to the mountaintop of Prayer and Hope, that they may plead for thee — then dash them to the valley of despair, the floor of which is covered with the stones of sacrifice and grief.

So dead art thou to all but love of self thou dost not see that thou hast also fallen with thy victims and nevermore shalt rise 'till every sacrificial stone which holds thy prey shall enter sentient life and cry to Heaven to help thee rise.

Long, long the eons are, and yet thou hast not learned to treasure any gift the gods have made, and suffered sore in giving.

Long, long the ages. Still thou throwest Love's most precious gifts upon the stones of sacrifice — 'twixt whiles thou raisest hands to heaven and pleadingly doth beg for more and greater gifts.

THE VICTOR

Think not to gird the laurel leaves of earthly fame upon the brow of him whom countless hosts of light hail "Victor" in life's lists. What careth such as he for "Things," — for sense illusions?

Alone, unheralded, a neophyte he comes upon the screen of time. Alone he lives and dies. Purified by fire, bereft of pride, alone he must ascend the steps strewn with the vanquished and the slain of long past days.

Each hard-fought vantage ground he wins gives footing to another soul, who, hard beset, doth follow him. Each plunge into the stream which gushes from the fountain head doth shower with cleansing drops some weary one too weak to reach their source.

The homage of thine heart will strengthen him for future battles with the hostile dwellers on the path who fain would stop him on the way. Thy love may give him courage to endure unto the end. For, know ye now, he may not lay his arms aside to crown himself until you, too, have reached the goal; a conqueror in truth.

YOUR HOURS

"The hours behind thee are God's hours, the hours before thee are His secrets. This hour alone is thine. Waste not your hour." So cries the Persian Muezzin[1] at dawn.

Are the hours behind thee hours of procrastination and self-indulgence? If so, the hours before thee will be those of sighing for lost opportunity. Wilt thou, then, let the present hour slip by in futile planning, over-confidence or indecision?

Happy he who sees and grasps the chances life and effort bring to him and weaves them in a chaplet for his brow.

THE CYCLIC ROUNDS

If thou lovest thyself, then art thou slave to thyself. If thou lovest thy brother, then art thou slave to thy brother — but through thy slavery to thy brother shalt thou find release from thy slavery to self. For, loving thy brother, thou lovest God, and only in love of God canst thou find eternal freedom from bondage to self.

Out of the Darkness cometh Light. Out of Light cometh Life. Out of Life cometh Death. Out of Death cometh Darkness, and out of Darkness cometh Light.

---

[1] *Muezzin (Arabic)* — a man who calls Muslims to prayer five times a day from the minaret of a mosque.

So, out of slavery to self cometh freedom to thy brother. Out of thy brother's freedom cometh slavery to thee. Out of that slavery cometh *eternal* freedom for both thee and thy brother.

Life and Death, Darkness and Light, Freedom and Slavery, Love and Hate; Round after Round, Cycle after Cycle, even as the spokes of a wheel fly round from night unto day and from day unto night.

THE UMBILICUS

THE path between Gods and men is the umbilicus which once connected God and man. The navel, the Central Spiritual Sim, is the point of separation between Spirit and Matter. The umbilicus connection was severed when the Elohim[1] said, let us make man in our own image, and having so made man they set him down in the Garden of Eden. Man himself cut the cord between him and the great Father-Mother, therefore man must reunite the two severed ends of the cord. This is the real occult secret behind the use of the navel in concentration by some of the ancient teachers. Symbolically it is the lower end of the Path. The gateway, so to speak; and if the gateway is choked by weeds (sensuous desires and gratifications), the soul cannot pass through it to reach the path of true knowledge and power.

LIFE'S DEMAND

THE power of the Seventh-sphere Gods; the concentrated rays of a golden sun formed into disks and marked with a sign. The jewels of a star-decked sky; the lamps which light a world at dusk; the common use of the life streams which are great enough to whirl the planets in space.

All these thou demandest of life, thou puny man of a single hour out of the eternities of time.

"But the price to be paid is too high," ye shamefacedly whine, though all that life demands of thee in return is — respect for thy

---

[1] *Elohim* (*Hebrew*) — a name for God in the Hebrew Scriptures.

creators; recognition of the rights of the weak; loving service for thy kind. Truly, much may be given for little.

THE CROWN

SINCE dawned the first new day — the day when woman stood beside her mate and for his glory parted with the crown of her supremacy, has woman sacrificed her life, her all, upon the altars raised by man.

And always, to the end of time, will woman light the fires and lay her sacrifices down to be consumed upon those man-made altars. It is the law, the law invoked by yielding crown for chain. It is her glory and her shame. It is the price she pays for love, and love is the last offering she lays on the sacrificial pile.

But time will cease and life be lost in Love eternal. Man and woman both — the two in one — shall wear the crown of immortality when dawns the next new day.

JUST SO FAR

WHEN man can find no word of good to say of fellowmen; when sun and stars are darkened to his inward sight and all the world seems but a charnel house to him; when to his sick and morbid mind every woman is a wanton and every man a cheat, and little children shrink, soul-warned, away from him — then art thou justified in placing all the earth 'twixt him and thee. Deadlier far is he to thee than any untamed beast.

When woman, formed of finest attributes of God, can stoop to bare a sister's sorrow or her shame to satisfy her thirst for vengeance, jealousy or rage; when envy or ambition blinds her inner eye and places in her breast a stone where there should beat a heart; when passion overcomes compassion and plots to gain desire by slaying friendship, gratitude and loyalty to kith and kin — then climb the skies or seek the ocean's bed if nowhere else is hiding place for thee. The very breath thou drawest in such presence is foul and tainted. A scorpion's sting may be withdrawn, but naught can draw the poison from the wounds an evil woman makes.

So far as every true and loving heart of womankind may reach toward God, so far as every Christlike, noble man may follow her — e'en just so far doth every faithless, poison-tainted woman fall toward the depths of non-existence, and every demon-driven man skulk in her footsteps.

THE FATHER'S CARE

LONG ere father, mother, wife or husband folded thee in love or bound thee with the ties of duty, I have watched o'er thee and led thee through the paths of sky and underworld; oft waited on the threshold of some den where thieves had spread a net and caught and held thee until thy voice in anguish fell upon my ear; then plucked thee forth as man doth pluck a brand from fire; oft snatched thee back from crater's mouth and serpent's fangs, and held thee safe against my breast 'til strength and courage came again to thee.

Yet thou canst idly stand and see the vandal hand tear down the home that sheltered thee when homeless, the arms left empty which had held thee close when thou wert lone and friendless: canst see my body thrown into the tiger's jaws, or hold my hands the while an enemy doth snatch the poison from the viper's fangs, and thrust it in the wounds made in my flesh while guarding thee.

Poor, tried and feeble offspring of a poorer race! There comes a day when thou wilt learn of higher Mother-Fatherhood, of purer, stronger love than that of wife or husband, friend or lover; a claim upon your fealty far more exacting than any claim now made on thee.

When comes that day, then thou wilt see that thou wert false to all that held thy love, by being false to love's own self, and must retrace thy steps if thou wouldst find the long lost path which leads to the abode of Love — the place of Recognition, Service, and Divine Compassion.

THE LOAD

Not all the Devas of the upper worlds can force the Devas of the underworld to face the Asuras[1] at the gate of Power against their will. No more can man be forced to enter that same gate against his will. If he be frighted at the flames or swept to one side by the waters as he enters the gateway, or if he make answer, "'tis my brothers' sin, I am guiltless," when the thunders of "the Voice" proclaim his own or his brothers' offenses against the law, then surely will the flames enwrap him and the waters o'erwhelm him.

Only through the brother he hath so wronged, may that gate be opened once again to him for he hath not borne his share of the burden taken up by both him and his brother when both lay in the womb of duration. In leaving that brother to bear that burden alone, he hath shifted the whole load to his own shoulders and the size and weight of the burden hinders swift passage through the gateway where first gather the flames and waters of the Path.

WOULDST THOU WIN?

Is thine own heart so pure and free from stain that thy brother's sin looms darkly on its white surface when reflected thereon? If so thou thinkest, then art thou under Maya's sway.

Wouldst thou win to mastery? Then write thy brother's offenses in water and thine own in fire. The water will extinguish the fire, the fire will raise the water to vapor, and both thine own offenses and thy brother's also will disappear.

---

[1] *Asuras* (*Sanskrit*, "breath") — exoterically, elementals and evil gods, considered maleficent; demons and no-gods.

THE FEAST

MAN'S usurpation of the prerogatives of God, and indifference to his own when they are related to his kinship with that of God, holds him to a steady diet of the husks of life which are only fit for swine.

He lifts up his eyes to his Father from afar, but makes no self-conscious effort to cross the barrier he himself has created between his Father and himself or to reach the table on which the holy Feast is spread for him alone, awaiting his coming, until, driven from his retreat by the very swine he has robbed, he stands face to face with utter starvation.

Then, naked and ashamed, he makes one last supreme effort to tear down the barrier and reach the heavenly food, and learns that there is no barrier; that it was long since raised by the hand of God and all that was required of him was to seat himself on the divan and dip his hand in the dish.

THY BONDS

THINKEST thou to forge a chain to bind thy brother's life to thine and yet go free from any act of his?

If so, a sad surprise awaits thee at the end. Every act of man with good or ill intent, doth form a link in the long chain of consequences which binds the human race in bonds of Time.

Not e'en a shadow cast by thee departs for aye. And if it falls athwart the vision of thy brother it will return in some far distant day to cloud thy vision, as thou didst cloud thy brother's.

And if thou bind thy brother purposely to thee with ill intent, no further act of thine can loose the bond. Unseen, unfelt by thee, it may remain for long, but one day fate will draw it taut, and struggle as thou wilt, thou canst not loose thyself. The bond alone may break the chain with which he hath been bound.

YOUR RESPONSIBILITY

THERE is some one person next in line to you upon the evolutionary ladder on which you stand, who is waiting for you to give the hand which will lift him to your side, and you will be held accountable to some degree if he fall from his present position to a lower round.

Knowing this, how dare you rest supinely on your supporting step and make no effort to bring that one into the Temple light? No amount of reason or logic will help you to locate that one. You will not know who and what he is until he stands by your side in some initiation.

The law which controls the influence lines also governs nature's method of combination and correlation of minutiae and mass. Your voice may not reach the ears and affect the conduct of many people at once, but it will reach the ears and turn the heart of the one who is waiting, if you voice the message you yourself have received from some agent of the Great White Lodge.

LIFE KNOTS

IF THOU wouldst attain to Wisdom's heights, then turn thy face toward that Sun whose rays are fastened in the hearts of living things, as knots are fastened at the end of threads, which serve to make or mend the garments worn by man.

No cunning finger ever can unloose the knots which God has tied. The garment made of flesh may fall away, but ever doth the knot remain to fasten newer, fresher garments as they form in turn. For in the knots so tied doth lie the root from which all sentient life proceeds.

FULFILLMENT BY FAITH

WHEN Faith waits patiently on Fulfillment, Fulfillment well justifies Faith. Doubt madly rushes unbelief and unbelief kills Faith aborning.

Believe in your God, yourself, your ideals, and live forever. Doubt your God, yourself, your ideals, and die to Truth.

Doubt arrogantly turns it back on Faith and loses itself in a maelstrom of despair. Truth glimpses a star, aims direct and reaches that star.

No man can believe a lie, though he may deceive himself as to his belief in that lie.

Belief lives only in Truth. Faith and Belief are lovers; Doubt and Unbelief are rivals for the hand of Despair.

MY GIFTS TO THEE

I GAVE thee thy heart's desire, brought from afar and laid at thy door; I gave thee wine and oil of spiritual life to build up the waste and barren places of thy Soul that it might live and bring thee compensation for the past.

Unmindful of the opportunity to share whate'er of value came to thee in recompense, as ever hath been done by all Earth's tried and tested ones, thou, having eaten of the fruit now fling the refuse to the skies.

CAUSE AND EFFECT

CAN man enter again his mother's womb, to be born again into physical life? Can man enter the womb of spiritual life for a new birth, if he hath destroyed the fertility of the seed from which that life unfolds?

Neither ignorance nor carnal desire can alter the law of cause and effect. He who throws away his sustenance of body or of soul must starve and die. He who conserves and cherishes that sustenance hath always a full supply which, like the widow's cruse, the gods replenish day by day.

THE GREAT MOMENT

To the soul who is capable of a great love there comes a moment of illumination when the veil between spirit and matter is lifted and it catches a glimpse of the tragedy which lies beyond the present time and dimly feels its approach.

Every great love bears the seed of a deep tragedy. It is seldom understood or appreciated by its recipient and seldom returned.

In that moment of illumination the soul knows beyond any shadow of doubt that the great tragedy of vicarious atonement, of sacrifice beyond power of expression, awaits it also as it has awaited all other souls at some period of their manifestation. But the veil falls quickly, the shadows flee, and again the great light sheds its beams over all common things, dazzling the intellect and magically endowing the beloved one with the attributes of a god.

And so the soul passes on to its Gethsemane and Golgotha to pay the price demanded by Divine Law.

COME

A voice said "Come!" and out from the darkness of unbelief, the shadow of death, I passed to glory like unto the sun, to the peace of the delivered. But I passed through waters wild and deep, I was beset by foes on every side; I stumbled, fell and rose again, still pressing on. Ear away upon the path the whispered "come" echoed and re-echoed. When I stumbled or fell, its power surrounded, held and raised me to my feet; when the shadows deepened and I could not see my way, in fiery letters just before my face I saw the word "come," and followed on. The end is yet far off, but fear has gone, and ever and anon I hear a whisper soft and clear which bids me "come," and though I weary and grow exceeding faint I cannot stop, I must go on until I no more hear that word, for then I shall have reached its source — my Home.

THE BEAUTIFUL MESSAGE

A PURE soul stood on the shore of the Ocean of Manifested Life waiting the final plunge that must bring oblivion of past glory — yet thrilling with rapture as memory recalled the message of glad tidings of which it was to be the bearer to the prisoned souls on the far distant shore.

The Lord of Life and Death drew near — and as the Soul lifted its arms for the last plunge, He threw over it a stainless mantle of purity. As the waves of that ocean rolled back, and the Soul finally stood on the nether shore, the shimmering light of that radiant garment caught the eyes of the waiting souls, and the contrast between it and the vile robes in which they were bound, maddened them. Jealousy — cruel, deadly, as the poisoned fangs of a serpent, awoke in their hearts; they could not wrest the garment from its wearer, but one by one they stooped and gathered handful after handful of slimy mud, and with vengeful spite hurled it over the garment, regardless of the fact that their own hands and robes had become soiled and filthy from contact with that mud.

Hounded on from one spot to another, its wings broken, its garment in shreds, and vile past telling — striving to give the beautiful message it bore to those whose shrieks of laughter and despair drowned the words ere they passed the trembling lips, the one white soul crept back to the waters whence it came, and as it sank on the sands, the same wave that brought it thither lifted it up and bore it back to the Lord of Life and Death. Lifting it to His breast, the Lord said: "Thou, water, which hast cleansed my garment, take back the mud thou bearest, to that nether shore. The prisoned souls shall be drenched with that mud until such time as they shall have caught my message with their own ears."

HIS BIRTHRIGHT

POOR soul-starved, heart-hungry children, huddled as sheep in a pasture, in some corner of a great city where never a glimpse of Nature's beautiful face meets your eye, where never a sound of the grand undertones of the billow-tossed ocean falls upon your ear.

The silence and peace of our brooding mother Night throws open to longing eyes, dim visions of spangled folds of that sable garment in which she was clothed herself while she whispers to the restless, storm tossed soul, "Be still, my child, and learn of me; lay your weary head burdened with care, maddened by pain, upon my breast, while I murmur the lullaby which has hushed you to sleep again and again in the long past ages."

Those strange, cold stars with their shadowy gleams of light thrill us by their mystery; they seem as the eyes of the Infinite searching our hearts for hidden evils, yet calming, steadying, strengthening every good impulse and bringing us into tune with the great major chord of Eternal Love — imparting a sense of courage and hope that not even the carking care of the work-a-day world can rob us of entirely.

Sometimes our agony is too deep, too real, for words; we have reached our Golgotha and can only lie on that great Mother-heart and moan, while she presses her fingers upon our eyes and gradually draws us into a presence far greater than her own — a Presence, the light of which floods us with glory unspeakable — a glory in which we are finally lost as is a drop of water in an ocean, and only awaken to know that our agony and pain were angels sent to bring us eternal blessedness.

O could you but realize what you lose when you permit the present mad rush for city life to engulf you, soul and body, and set you down where the clang and clatter of machinery, the babel of human noises, allow you never a moment for the silence which is as necessary to the soul as is food to the body.

Surely there is a great undercurrent of wisdom in the words now finding an echo in the hearts of the people, in the words, "Back to the soil"; fit refrain for an army of toilers returning to claim their own. For when mankind deserts the land to crowd into the cities, it gives up its birthright for the husks of life.

LOVE IS GOD

IF THE lips, now sealed by the Angel of Death, might unclose and permit the spirit now hovering near to speak in earthly tones, it would say, "Behold, I that was dead am alive forevermore. The gates of Hell are closed behind me, and I have entered into mine inheritance. Wherefore do ye weep for me?

"There is no death, my beloved, nothing but life, life, life, everywhere and forever.

"What matters it that ye lay down my body, a worn-out shell, an empty chrysalis, that so my Tight be not impeded? For I go to the place prepared for me, radiant with joy, full of that peace that passeth understanding. Be patient with me yet awhile that I leave thee in loneliness, and let not the delusion of space blind thee to the truth that thou art with me, though thou knowest it not — for nothing can separate souls bound by love. They are entwined by the force of that love with bonds far stronger than those of earth — for Love is God. 'Blessed are ye that mourn, for ye shall be comforted.' Lift up your gates, and the King of Glory shall come in!"

Those gates of the body which close the portals of the soul before all weary eyes, eyes that will not unclose for the King of Glory to enter until their lids are raised by the power of intuition, or beaten down by the Angel of Death. "Show me a dead thing," said a Sage, "and I will destroy the whole doctrine of immortality?" Is this a vain boast, or a promise of eternal joy?

COME FORTH THOU CHRIST

COME forth. O thou who livest as does Thought in the eternal heart of God — thou Christ of God, come forth to bless this Star we call our home, for yet thou art not manifest to holden human eyes.

Sly spirit broods in ecstasy of pain o'er that ideal of Thee which is my life, my hope, my all.

Springing from the fathomless, the mystery of life and love, again shalt Thou in power and glory stand upon the threshold of this world and beckon to Thee.

And quickly will I kneel before Thy Grace, Thy Truth and Beauty, beseeching that Thy hand may for a moment rest on my bowed head to still the longing of my soul, which, smothered in agony of yearning love, can now but beat its wings against this earthly cage, unable to escape or patiently endure.

Through all the world my weary feet have strayed — on highest mountaintop, in vale and in clefts of rock, in deepest caverns underneath the earth, searching, ever searching, for a clue to guide me unto Thee — until I have grown old and feeble in the quest. But God can never die, and Thou art God and God is Love, and in the deepest recesses of soul I feel that I shall yet behold Thee with mine eyes. For love like mine must meet response from Love like Thine, and Thou shalt bid this thought of mine which dwelleth yet within Thy heart — this great ideal of all the human race — to leave its hiding for a space and come to us, to all that wait and pray.

THE SONG OF LIFE

Soul of my soul, do you hear it? Listen! Do you hear the mad music of clarion and flute, of fife and drum — the pounding on pavement of marching steps — the cry, "To Arms!" through the city streets — the bugle-call through byway and lane? Do you hear the wild gallop of horses' hoofs, the shriek of the smitten, the dirges of death?

Do you hear the mad revel of wine and song, the tripping and sliding of dancing feet — the maniacal screams of frenzied men? Do you hear them, those echoes of hell on earth?

Do you hear it, soul of my soul — hear the sweet song of the Bird of Life, as it swells and soars, and pierces that loathsome night, calling you, thrilling, saddening, yet gladdening you; inciting to joy so near akin to pain — the ever growing mystery appalls you! Do you hear it cleave the vibrant waves of hell's domain, as the arms of a strong man cleave the waters engulfing him, flecking with radiant light all hearts attuned to its low measure, as foam from the ocean flecks the open face of day?

All the waters of all the earths cannot drown it: all the fires of all the hells cannot separate it from you. You alone of all earth's myriad creatures can muffle that sweet song, can interpose a single obstacle to its passage to and from the ears of your own heart.

THE MESSAGE

A TERRIFIC crash of thunder rent the midnight air, sending great waves of sound reverberating from one end of the heavens to the other. A great pulsating globe of fire, much like a sun, appeared in the far distance. From it, in every direction, were darting broad, zigzag streams of lightning, which seemed to pierce the very ends of the universe. From the globe of fire there issued a voice that at first sounded like the low mutterings of thunder, but on closely listening could be distinguished in slow, deep, penetrating tones the words: "Write to the stillborn sons of Earth." Then came the message given below:

"Dwarfed are ye, ye sons of Earth who once were great enough to tread the burning sands of Rapa Nui,[1] and with your own bared hands pile up the statues of the Gods — ye whose minds conceived the Holy Temples lying now full forty fathoms 'neath old ocean's waves.

Ah, but ye have fallen low, and when mine eyes behold your puny forms, your sordid minds, I see how great the fall, how slow the rising from the depths of your disgrace and punishment.

Can nothing rouse ye from your sleep to knowledge of the truth that ye are Sons of God, as well as earthen vessels? Must hoary cycle tread upon the heels of cycles past, and ye lie still and make no move to climb the heights where once ye had a dwelling place with Devas fair and wise?

---

[1] *Rapa Nui* — Easter Island, located in the southeastern Pacific Ocean. There are mysterious sculptures that testify to the existence of the ancient civilization of the Lemurians, a race of giants.

Will neither sad entreaty nor scornful lashings of a pointed tongue goad you on to grasp once more the heritage which alien hands have wrested from your grasp?

Day crieth unto Day and Night moans unto Night, and ye lie wrapt in Lethe's false embrace, or for a golden chain, a Ruby rare and precious to your clouded sight, relinquish all the power and wealth which lieth now unclaimed amidst the treasures of your Father's house.

Waken! Waken! Waken! Slothful child of earth, stretch out thy palsied arm and strive to grasp the hand outstretched to thee. Straighten the limbs now stiff and curled beneath thy form, and strive to reach the path which leads to the great Eye upon the Mountaintop: for night is coming on, in which no man may work, and if thou canst not work, there is no place for thee upon the earth where Service is the law of life, the chiefest blessing left to fallen man, the Pledge of final union 'twixt thy God and thee, which thou hast bartered now and must reclaim ere thou canst Wisdom find and know."

THE TASK

MY CHILD: If thou wouldst bear the colors of the Lodge, then stand alone. Search thine own heart, lay bare its hidden motives, follow thou the dictates of its will. Take care lest any thing or creature bind thy course of action, yet make thou sure that thing or creature occupies its rightful place in all thy plans where it is equally concerned with thee.

No human soul hath earned the right to bind *another* soul, yet every soul must bind itself to serve the soul that rightfully demands its help.

We fear to trust the guiding power of Love — the God within — lest being haled before the Judgment seat, we stand rebuked for failure to perform *aright* the task imposed by Love, and in that failure sink the right to say: "I only did what thou commandedst me."

THE LITTLE THINGS

WOULDST thou know the secret of a happy life? Then come aside with me into the great white Silence and I will show thee strange things. Strange to thee in that thou hast passed them by openly day by day and year by year, yet hast never paused to look upon their faces. When thou hast come anigh them thou hast trampled them underfoot, in ignorance of their worth, or covered them with refuse. They did not appear seemly in thine eyes, for truly their forms were unsightly, their eyes cast down, and their tiny bodies, like stinging insects, came between thee and the light of the sun. Thou couldst not see that they brought thee rare treasure, great opportunities, to add to thy store of riches till thou shouldst become of all men most to be envied.

The small worries, the trifling cares, the quick, harsh word of a neighbor, all the little things which much thought and anxiety enlarge to portentous sizes. It is these that eat into thy life, that line thy face, that sear and callous thy heart. The great sorrows, great tribulations and losses sweeten and strengthen thee, yet can do so no more than may the little things, if thou wouldst but stop, lift up their heads and gaze into their beautiful, downcast eyes; downcast, for they hold a message for thee none other may read.

THE PRICE

SO LONG as fear of poverty, of death or suffering can influence you to withhold the whole or even a part of the price demanded by the law for your perfect development, you will never cross the threshold of the Great Initiation Chamber. So long as you retain any part or feature of the great renunciation *when offered by you* to the Lodge of Life, that part or feature will chain you to the Cosmic Wheel, a victim of jour own selfishness and dishonesty. As Ananias and Sapphira[1] lost life and belongings through willful perversion of the law, so every Chela of the Lodge who has demanded

---
[1] *Ananias and Sapphira* — a couple in the New Testament who suddenly died after they lied (see Acts 5:1–11).

the service, love and devotion of the Masters in exchange for the service, obedience and love they offer, and who then undertake to withhold a part of the offering, must inevitably return to the diet of husks, the swine — selfish elements — are nourished upon.

So long as your demands remain unanswered, and your desire for the husks is unappeased, if you will be content to remain with the swineherd, the higher law will not reach you; but you cannot wallow in the filth of the pen and treasure the husks, and at the same time stand before the bright flash of the Sword of the Spirit without being cloven in two.

The choice is yours; but, having made the choice, you must bear the results. God will have no divided hearts. It is quite possible that Karmic Law[1] will not accept a full relinquishment of all you hold dear, even when cheerfully offered, but so long as attachment to any thing or creature prevents you from freely offering up that thing or creature upon the altar of devotion, the Holy Fire cannot descend and touch that offering, and thereby render it of use. And the lower fires which form such attachments must eventually consume the things to which you are attached, and leave you desolate and comfortless. Make no offer to the Law which you are not fully prepared to have accepted. Keep all you have and are if such be your desire, but in keeping it, remain on the outside of your own divinity.

THE POWER OF LOVING

WHAT matters it that form and face of thy beloved grow feeble, old and wrinkled? What matters it that the shell which held thy love shall be in time a feeding place for worms, or even that lust and all uncleanness shall leave their imprint on the face that thou hast pressed against thine own in ecstasy of pain? The soul that thus expressed itself in form, that part of thee and me which drew and called to active life the sleeping Love of Life

---

[1] *Karmic Law* — the law of equilibrium, of adjustment. When equilibrium is disturbed, action and reaction take place until perfect balance or harmony is again attained.

dwells not in form or face of any living thing, though in thy blindness thou wouldst so confine it.

Look o'er the pages of thy life — the pages of the open book writ by the hand of God, and thou shalt find that like as thou hast grown to man's estate by slowly filling in the heavenly pattern of thyself, day by day, so hath thy *power of loving* grown, and yet may grow to compass all the spheres of life.

That thing or creature thou didst love with all the power thou hadst when but a child, no longer charms thine eye, though in that charm didst truly manifest a soul that after many years again shone through a fleshly form and face which drew and held thee fast; and so again shall love increase and search the heavens to find itself.

When all the lower fires of personal possession shall burn themselves away, then thou wilt find in every human face, in flower and tree, in wind and water, in all things and creatures, and finding never lose again, the flawless soul that thou hast always loved, and find it waiting the glad hour when every note of all the wondrous Song of Life shall sound forth pure and sweet for all who list to hear.

TWILIGHT AND DAWN

WHEN thy fellow-pilgrims turn from fulsome praise and adulation to harshest criticism and vilification of the bearer of the torch who is blazing a trail through the dense growth of the underworld, that he may find the Path, if thou wilt not be turned from thine allegiance, look well that the moss entwined stump of selfish desire o'er which thy brother has stumbled doth not trip thee also. Walk warily, lest the half-buried rocks of ambition or jealous rage catch thy feet and hold thee captive by his side.

One extreme of life always calls to the other, and it must respond. If thou wouldst travel the trail of safety, keep well in the middle of that trail. The light of the torch borne before thee throws flickering shadows on either side of the trail, but burns clear and bright on the central line.

Twilight must follow day. Night doth not drop its sable curtain in an instant. Dawn doth *silver* the darkness of night e'er the Sun doth turn that darkness into gold.

So always, Twilight and Dawn, silvered darkness and golden light, are hours of consecration — are always places of Peace wherein the soul may pause in the midst of clamor to catch a note of the Song of Life and clear its point of vision if it but walk in the line of unwavering Truth.

YOU MUST CHOOSE

Love's little ones, and therefore mine, I pray you open wide the closed and bolted doors behind which now you sit in apathy, and let my words of tenderness gain access to your hearts; those doors that you have girded round about with iron bands and locked with golden locks, and paneled with the dross of baser metals. Let me in, that I may serve to help you drive the demons forth which you unwittingly enthrone in places which the gods alone should hold — the demons of your pride of intellect, contempt and love of adulation. Fear not that I shall seize upon the treasures of the Soul, for are you not mine own? And shall I rob myself? I long to lead you from the paths of loneliness, of poverty and weakness — Maya's gifts, which you, all unwitting of their nature, now so eagerly accept.

With arms outstretched I cry to you and stand aghast at your indifference to the cry, and at my lack of power to pierce the aura of the world's delusions in which you are encased. The demons of unholy fire, of water and of air, aroused to fury now, and fed by man's inhuman acts, are piling up their barriers of brands 'twixt you and those who fain would serve you, e'en while you meekly bring your quota of the brands and throw them, wearily, upon the pile. The crackling of the flames, the muttering of the distant storm, fall on your deadened ears, while here and there a great red drop falls from low lying clouds and splashes on the earth or drenches some poor heart with life's woe.

The disembodied fiends so long restrained, have broken loose, and now are seizing upon the newborn vehicles of weak, impotent souls, thus gaining instruments for use in the great conflict, and yet you fail to know them even when yourselves have furnished them with vehicles — you are so taken up with some side issue, some secondary thing, which of necessity must fall in its own place when once the primal, the composite issue is fully recognized and holds its own.

The war is on 'twixt right and wrong, 'twixt heaven and hell, and you must choose your side.

THE WILL TO LIVE

As breaks the long, low rumble of the surf-bound shore upon the outer ear, and so accustoms it to Nature's lowest register of tone that it is dulled to all the sweeter, softer notes of rippling brook and hum of busy insect, so the loud thunder of the unbound passions, the shrieks of mad, unsatisfied Desire doth dull, the inner ear of man, and will not let him hear the Soul's low cry for help to find its own, its triple chord, now lost amidst the myriad sounds which beat the ether into waves that break upon the shores of sentient life in ever widening curves, carrying on their crests or in the silent depths beneath, the missing tones which wait the sounding of the key; that key which only can be heard when all the discords, all the harsher sounds of life are stilled.

All naked and alone, bereft of hope and plunged into abysmal depths where light nor sound may penetrate, that lonely soul must wander incomplete, its smothered wail the only outlet for its woe. No power it hath to sound the key, recalling the lost notes, and so completing the sweet chord which with its volume, strength and power would clothe that Soul with light and hope divine. For, losing those sweet tones in Passion's drear domains, o'er which insatiable Desire hath rule, it loses e'en the power to make a plea for help, and so unceasingly it wanders on alone till myriad cycles pass, when once again it mingles with the maze of unborn Souls that wait the sounding of a higher key than that which rung its birth, and which will call to active life the dead and sleeping, and the embryos, the other victims of the greater Self — the *Will to live*.

LOOSE HIM

"Loose him and let him go." Unwind the swaddlings which you have wrapped about your brother man.

Your dogmas, creeds and penances, your selfish love as well as hate, are chains which bind you to the "Wheel of Woe."

Forgive the debts, undo the chains you bound your brother with in duty's guise. Loose him and let him go, and thou shalt find, not all the chains, the debts, the bonds with which you hold your friend in thrall will draw and hold him fast to you as will the knowledge he is free. Free to wander where he will, free to come and go, free to give you love for love, or to refuse e'en friendship's trove.

Each thread of every cord you use to bind another soul will bind *you* back, will hold *from you* the love you crave, the service you require.

In Freedom lies thy strength, and Freedom is the Law of Life; not liberty to hurt or crush another part of God's own life, but liberty to render service pure, and learn to find in strict obedience to law the goal of perfect life.

Obedience to law, through love of law and order, gives highest freedom to the soul; but man has put the bond of fear upon his brother man and so enslaved him to Illusion, and fear breeds naught but most abject subjection, and freezes into nothingness the slave, as well as he who doth enslave.

Obey implicitly the law of Love and thou shalt not be called upon to sacrifice aught save the thing thou needest not; but first be sure thou knowest Love, and hast not clothed it in the slimy garb of self-indulgence, thus paving wide the way for self-annihilation.

THE MILESTONES

Thus saith the Father to me, His child: As the stars in their courses fought against Sisera,[1] even so will I, the Lord thy God, fight against the stars if so be they lead mine own into the stronghold of the Great Shadow.

Even the stars are the work of my hands, and thou shalt not put the work of my hands in the seat of my power.

Thou art long in learning that the fierceness of my jealousy is the fierceness of the World-Mother who would protect her young from the poisonous fangs of the serpent; the fierceness of the jealousy of the father who refuses to deliver his only son to the maw of the hungry tiger, yet would gladly yield that son to satisfy the Higher Law; the fierceness of the jealousy which would sweep the dark stars from the skies did they bar the way to the heart of the least of my little ones.

Truly is it said, "All things work together for good to those who love God," but e'er thou canst interpret the promise aright, thou must learn to know the nature of such love as is demanded by thy God. What seemeth good to *thee* may be the settling of some shadow of a higher good, and in thy haste it may be thou wilt seize the shadow, wrap it closely round about thee, and so cut off the light by which alone the higher good may manifest to thee.

If e'en an angel host should bid thee turn from what thou knowest is the path of right, bid them turn about and seek the Father once again and so make sure they have not erred.

Far down that beautiful broad path the perfected have made 'twixt thee and me, doth also creep the wayward and the erring; and not all the words which fall upon thine ear — not all the sights which meet thine eyes, are for thy quick unfolding.

The pitcher which today is filled with pure and sparkling water from a living spring may ere another sun be set be filled

---

[1] *Sisera* — a commander of King Jabin's army, who oppressed the Israelites for twenty years. He was defeated in a battle with the forces of the Israelite tribes when even "the stars in their courses fought against Sisera" (Judges 5:20).

with poisoned wine, and all who drink thereof may meet an agonizing death. The milestones on the Path are plainly marked. The contents of the pitcher indicate their character. Why, then, be deceived, and let thy lack of patience, or thy greediness for power or place, or things of spirit or of body, lead thee into byways, or quench thy thirst with that which breeds a greater thirst and ends in death?

THE PEACE OF ALL FULFILLMENTS

YE RESTLESS wanderers of the worlds, who find no place on Earth or Sea or Sky on which to plant a foot and anchor there, those rapidly pulsating vehicles of the Soul you pamper or abuse at will, while seeking surcease from the stress and strain the Jinns have laid upon you.

Know ye not, when first you yielded to the driving power of Fohat which sent you forth on an unceasing search for Lethe's streams, or for the apples of Hesperides,[1] you opened wide the door which led into the closed and secret place of the soul; you wrenched apart the close-bound strands of that golden cord which held your Souls in leash that they might learn the lessons which a single point in space can teach as well and better far than all the leagues of Earth and Sea and Sky that you have traveled o'er? Heedlessly ye have invoked the restless elementals of the lower spheres to make their homes within your Souls. And they have now seized the reins of power and drive you round about according to their whims, that they may minister to their desire for ceaseless motion. Day by day your power of seeking Silence, Peace, and all that Wisdom born of consecrated effort, slowly wanes and leaves you tenfold more the slave you were. Your eyes are blinded by the dust satiety has flung therein, and like a ship with rudder gone and anchor buried fathoms deep beneath the ocean's wave, you drift about with ne'er a port in sight, in total ignorance of the truth that ye are but the sport of creatures you would cast derision

---

[1] *Apples of Hesperides* — in Greek mythology, the golden apples that granted immortality to those who ate them.

on, if once your eyes were opened to the light of your divinity and hidden power o'er lower forms of life. Wake up, tear off the bandage from your eyes, find your niche, and labor for your fellow-man, close fast those wide-flung doors, and seek the Silence and the Peace of all fulfillment.

YOUR DEFEATS

YOU gauge the value of what you deem your greatest achievements by the measure of success which has followed your strongest efforts, but in the days to come, when the mists have fallen from your eyes, and you sum up the results of your life work, you will find to your great surprise that the defeats which you have suffered, the blows which have bowed your heads the lowest, have always held the *real* values. Your successes may have taken you nearly to the Mount of Transfiguration, but your defeats will have carried you up and over the top of that mount.

THE SOUL REDEEMED

SWEETER than any song of thrush, softer than the wood-dove's coo to its mate, tender as the touch of dawn on the eyes of a sleep-bound child, falls the voice and touch of the Over-Soul[1] on the weary Pilgrim of Days.

Many times and oft in the night of the past hath he closed his eyes and said, "Surely my Lord will awaken me from this awful nightmare of Life ere another sun shall greet mine eyes. I am bound and helpless in the morass of the world's worst woe, and, alas, there are none to hear if I call, or drag me forth, for all of my kin are bound as am I, and smothered in viscid mud, while I alone of human kind am left with head above its slimy ooze."

---

[1] *Over-Soul* — the Universal Soul, also known as *Alaya* (*Sanskrit*, "abode"); the Father-Mother. All individual souls are its rays or sparks and are able to merge with it.

But e'en as he cried, lol the dark clouds parted, his feet were loosed, and with lightning speed an Angel came down and bade him rise and follow on, to the feet of the Lord of Life and Death.

At last fall the scales from the blinded eyes. In the glory of Soul redeemed stands he forth, poised on the earth like a bird on the wing. He asks of the sea, the sky and the earth, "Is it worth it all? Is it worth the anguish, the pain, the loss, to hear that voice, to feel that touch?" And from every fiber, from all live things, from the heavens and hells, in melody sweet, again and again, rises and echoes in vibrant tones, as with one great voice, the words of the saved: "Aye, it is worth all earth can give, all sun and moon and stars can offer."

LIGHT OF THE SOUL

THINKEST thou to win discrimination when, like a weathercock, thou veerest to one side or another according as the wind listeth?

Force thine unwilling feet, weighted with the mud of sense, to walk straightly in thy chosen path, that thou mayest quicker reach the golden light upon the mountaintop, and bathe thy soul in its pure radiance.

TO THE WORLD

DEGENERATE Scions of a dying Age! As a man freeth corruption from his nostrils, so will I cast you forth by the wind of my discontent. Back shall ye return to the darkness whence ye came — rebellious, quarrelsome, inhuman spawn of an evil age — abortions of my soul's travail, who will neither heed the moan of your own sad hearts or the thunderous waves of a nation's woe, lest greedy lust for place and power remain unsatisfied; lest your bodies — the feeding place of worms — be less daintily fed and clothed upon with fine raiment.

Long eons have I reached out to you in beseeching, and ye pass me by unheeding.

As breaketh forth the sweat o'er the straining muscles of the strong man, so outpour I the dew of my longing, and ye will not see nor listen.

Ye force the action of the Great Law upon your heads, and I, its minister, must needs serve, to your undoing.

LIFT THOU THINE EYES TO GOD

CHILD of The Eternal — listen! Know that though scorched by the sun of desert sands; lashed back by the furious ocean's waves; struck motionless by the power of the Ice-Angel, with the wings of thy soul as the wings of a bird when the Storm-King has beaten them close to its breast; know, son of the sun, even yet thou art not vanquished. Thou art more than conqueror through the illimitable love of that compassionate heart upon which thy head is pillowed. Cover thou thy breast with the shield of patience. Remember — the burning heat of the noontide glides slowly, imperceptibly, into the cool of evening. The mountain glaciers melt in the warmth of Spring and, drop by drop, water the thirsty valley below. Earth and sky meet and kiss in a blaze of unspeakable glory. And thou, son of my heart, though cast in the depths of depravity, weakness, or weariness, may rise to immeasurable heights, by lifting thine eyes to God.

Say not, "I am but a leaf in the wind." Say, rather, "I am of God — in God."

THE ETERNAL WARFARE

AH, MYSTERY of Life, mystery of Death, mystery of Evil! Only Infinite Love can sound your depths. Only Faith can impart the power by which a glimpse of that Love may be seen. Man is always at war with himself. He unfolds a flag of truce now and then when the battle becomes so fierce that mind, sense or physical power is on the verge of collapse, till he regains his breath and starts in again. And this continual battle is an absolute necessity, for only through it can he win his crown of power and endurance. Man could not live with himself on any other terms.

THE WHEEL OF SUFFERING

THE wrongs done to or against you by others may be made stepping stones for you, if you have the courage to lift your feet high enough from the ground to reach them. So long as a wrong can embitter you, and so long as you attract the commission of such wrongs, either by wronging others, or by personal limitations of any character, the invincible power of love will hold you to the wheel of suffering.

It takes poor, struggling humanity long, long ages to learn that divine Justice will never suffer a wrong to be done which is not at the same time a punishment for a similar wrong, and a vast opportunity to wipe out a debt.

The stronger, the better equipped for service is the Neophyte, the greater will be his or her tests of patience, endurance and compassion. The very attributes which make him useful and valuable to the Temple work, and therefore to the world, at the same time must bring long seasons of heart hunger, trial and mental strain, until he, like all those who tread the same path, can lay his burden in the lap of the Great Mother, and say from his heart, "It matters not what my brother, my sister may do to me, only give me more love for them, and I am content."

"I can safely leave the punishment of any offense done to me to the Divine Law, but woe is me, if I dwell with delight upon the nature, and application of that punishment, for by so doing I lift my head from the Mother's lap, and gaze into the eyes of the avenger of mine own offense."

THE PAIN OF PROGRESS

Force not the hand of Nature, lest you stir to action such antagonistic forces as now lie inert or sleeping, and so deliberately draw down upon your head that which as yet is but a formless fear and dread of coming evil.

Grasp with firm and steady hand devotion's sieve that holdeth thy life's happiness aloft; a single careless, trembling touch and lo! the finest grains are shaken through the meshes, and blown hither and yon by the first fierce wind of selfish longing, leaving naught but the coarse and weighty sands of satiated pleasure.

No man ascends towards the stars without arousing the ire of the yelping curs of earth.

THE GARDEN OF THE SOUL

Stop, weary, sun-smitten traveler o'er the desert sands of ages past! Rest ye awhile where the broad leaves of the trees that grow in the Garden of the Soul may fan thy fevered brow. List to the Song of Life, rising and falling, cleaving the air, trilling in ecstasy, melting in sweetness, as it ripples from the swelling throat of the Bird of Hope. Heed not the words of the Spirit of Death, re-echoing along thy backward track, where "Hope lay dead and Life was not worth the living."

Only the *dead* in *Life*, the heartless devotees of the Calf of Gold, which standeth knee deep in thine own and thy Brother's blood, may say in truth that Hope for them is dead.

Thou — beloved — who art only aweary, come with Me into the Garden of the Soul and rest, till thine eyes canst behold and bear the Light of Life.

RELIGHT THY TORCH

KNOW ye not, weary, disappointed, rebellious child of the Master — thou in whose heart, faith, hope and ambition languish and die through thy Brother's sin or failure — that thou alone art responsible for the effect of that failure upon thyself? For thou alone didst impart it power to hurt thee by accepting that which was but a means to the accomplishment of a great purpose, for the purpose itself.

Thine alone is the fault if thou dost not compel even that failure to assist thee in mounting the step beyond.

None other can harm thee, none other can hinder thy progress. Thou alone art the way to thy true self.

Rise up from the mire into which thou art thrown and travel onward. Mayhap thou shalt overtake thy Lord.

LIFE'S SHINE AND SHADOW

IF THE Path seem long and dark to you who look back on life's lessons from such a narrow point of consciousness, how think you it appears to us who, from the altitude of centuries of ceaseless labor, of hope deferred, still work on with the Law even when no light be visible? For know the radiant light of fulfilled purpose may not dawn for us until it dawns for you; we are all bound to the same wheel of change.

I, who would comfort you with my own comfort, can only bid you love more, hope more, trust more, work more — for, see, the first trembling rays from the newly risen Sun of Life even now gild the mountaintop, and the shifting shadows at its base partially reveal the glory to be made manifest when cyclic law has done its work.

Cast forth, then, the demon of discontent; it can undo in one day many years of toil; and, my children, do not forget that you yourselves have invoked your Karmic shadows, so be patient — even with the shadows.

THE ANGEL OF THE PATH

ONE day the earthly sun will darken before thine eyes. Naked and alone the Angel of the Path will thrust thee forth from the haunts of men to seek and find thine own, or to wander in dark places evermore in thralldom unto things.

Thyself a shadow, thou shalt come to Hades' shadowy vistas and with soft footfall glide from place to place, until thy soul's awakened eyes behold the blazing Arch of Triumph which separates that hell from heaven.

Then the stern Guardian standing there will say: "What bringest thou to me that I should let thee pass?"

None other gift than Love will he accept; all else he spurns as worthless chaff. So, gather thou each day the seeds from which Love sprouts — the kindly deed, the tender touch, or thou wilt be left standing on the farther side with only thy lost opportunities to think upon, thyself a shadow to the end.

THE LENS OF THE SOUL

BE NOT deceived. Only the pure in heart see God. Thou canst not defile the lens of thy soul by impure and selfish thought and behold the divine through such a medium. For the deceptive lights and shadows cast thereon do but hinder the reflections of aught higher than the false images pictured in thine heart, and thou art lost to all but the self-created mirage of false and fleeting vision where darkness seemeth as light — the darkness of Self in which no ray of the Divine Sun of Life can manifest its presence.

As a lily raiseth its head to the sun, so raise thou thy soul to God, that the dew of Divine Love may search out and help to uncover its hidden Heart of Gold.

THE LAW FULFILLED

BELIEVEST thou, O son of Earth's travail, that while the meanest serf remains a serf, thou canst be free? That while one child's low moan of pain ascends the spheres, pure joy may be thy portion?

Water seeks its level by a law divine. No less divine — unalterable, the law that makes thy brother's joy thy joy, that so the level of human bliss and agony be found, and wisdom justified.

If thou wouldst reach perfection, lift the stone that crushes to earth a tiny violet, a blade of grass. Bear with thy brother — share his weight of woe; pour of thine own abundance into his lap if he be needy.

Bind up the wound thine enemy received in strife with thee, and so aid in the final great adjustment of mortal man and things. The Law fulfilled will open up the path to God, now closed and barred by self.

JUDGE NOT

WHO — what art thou, delusion of evil, in the guise of man, that darest persecution of the Eternal, that rendereth false judgment upon the Absolute? God and Christ dwelleth in every atom of Substance, Force and Consciousness. Thou canst not lay a feather's weight of condemnation on another and let God and Christ go free.

Hidden within thine own heart is every evil thou imputest to thy brother. Destroy it in thyself and thou shalt never more behold it in thy brother.

UNSELFISH LOVE

MY CHILD: Canst thou not strive to consider the daily martyrdom of thy friend, thy wife, thy husband — the one that loves thee most unselfishly, the one to whom thou art as a star, however unworthy, however cold, careless and unloving in deed and truth — the one whose heart sings a song of sweetness throughout a hard day's toil — at a single kind or tender word from thee? O, blind and foolish one — thou who strivest with all thy power to lay up earthly treasures — all unthinking that the unselfish love of a human being for thee is thy opportunity for laying up priceless treasures throughout the ages to come.

THE INNER TEMPLE

IF ALL about thee seem to speak of sorrow, and the face of God is turned away from thee; if nowhere on the earth there seems to be a refuge for breaking hearts or minds unhinged by longing; if little children's cries awake the echoes in thine heart of long dead ages when the cries of other little ones ascended to the skies through sacrificial flames; if rest and peace have taken wings and flown away from thee and from thy kind; if music hath no longer charm, and art no solace, and the way to love seems closed to thee; if fear of death is swallowed up in fear of living, and all thy labor seems to be in vain — then come with me, my child. Keep close to me until thy search is ended, and thou hast reached the place of silence — place of peace — the Temple in thine inmost heart.

When thou shalt reach that Temple's door and knock *aright*, then shalt thou find it opening wide into the heart of every other living thing; and in some one of all those wondrous spaces shalt thou find the answers to thy hardest questions, and surcease from thy deepest woes.

Nowhere else upon the earth or in the heavens can the key be found that will unlock God's Jewel case; but on its burnished sides in deeply carven letters are the clues to that which lies within — and they are hidden in the words, *Faith, Hope, Service.*

CEASE, AND SING

CEASE your moaning and your wailing, ye enlisted soldiers of the Army of your God. Did ever soldier win his spurs, win command of battling legions, who at sight of guns and sabers, battlefields and wounds, fell out of line or cringed in terror and despair? Beat it into dull and sodden minds if ye needs must, that never was a just and righteous cause left undefended, nor was it lost for aye. Nay, not even if it sank from sight of man for days or years; not even if the last defender perished in the final battle fought; like a buried seed, in time, it sprang into a newer, higher life, tenfold the stronger, tenfold the surer of success for all the bloodshed, all the tears that watered its first growth.

What right have you to ride serenely on above the heads of those who fight, and never strike a blow yourself in your defense? Or that you should escape the common lot of men and soldiers fighting for a cause on which now rests the fate of nations yet unborn? Or that your limbs, the air you breathe, the flesh you bear, escape the reptile's coils and breath and fangs — the rank abuse, the slanderous tongues, the crushing of your hearts by coward's blows? Can you not bear what weaker men have bravely borne — the burden of their fellowmen — and hold your heads on high, and smile and sing? *Aye, sing so loud and strong that not a note of all the discord on the field below may strike your ear?*

All, if you can but do my bidding, then are you children of the King, soldiers of the cross of Christ — the symbol of eternal life for all the World. Then are you on the road that leads to where the Hosts of Light now stand and beckon you, the road to Mastery.

A CLARION CALL

FIGHT! For fight you *must*, you Children of the Covenant, or shirk the task set by your own Divine Self.

Look where you may, in all life's domains, no spot or place will meet your eye where battle doth not rage.

Would *you*, of all the myriad lives on earth, in cowardice cast down your shield, remove your armor, lie supinely down, and claim the fruits of all the labor, all the strife between the Sons of Light and the Brothers of the Shadow? Between *The Perfected* and all the Lethe-drunken scions of a dying age? And never strike a blow to prove yourself a worthy foe, or aid in the defense of all the right and privilege so hardly won? Can you refuse to guard the fortress and protect the overwearied, scarred and broken veterans whose right to longer fight has been denied, or guide the footsteps of the feeble and faint-hearted — the helpless "little ones"?

The hardest fight of all the ages past is *on*, and fight you *must* if you would pave the way for the return of those who fought in a lost cause and gave their lives that *you* might live and win the martyr's crown that they now wear — that crown which is an "open sesame" to all the Thrones — the Powers — of Heaven and Earth.

Gird tightly on your loose-worn weapons. Buckle fast your yet unsteady headpiece, and *strike*, while strike you may, at all the enemies entrenched in that frail heart of yours, and die, if die you must, with face turned toward the foe, content that life has given you a chance to fight, instead of swathing you with bands that hopelessly ensnare and hold the human soul.

Be great, because of that your greatness hath the power to overcome, and fight till victory is yours, and yours the right *to stand erect and unabashed before the very face of God.*

WARRIORS OF LIGHT

"Warriors of Light, Warriors of Truth, I salute you, in the name of the Great White Brotherhood. Go forth to battle, with the Powers of Darkness, armed with the Sword of the Spirit of God, the Breastplate of Righteousness, the Helmet of Eternal Truth. See to it, then, that no stain rest on that armor, no rust on that sword, that ye may become one with us, on that Great Day 'Be With Us.'"[1]

---

[1] *Great Day "Be With Us"* — the period of Rest. It corresponds to the Day of the Last Judgment. This is the day when man, freeing himself from the trammels of ignorance, and recognizing fully the non-separateness of the Ego within his Personality — erroneously regarded as his own — from the Universal Ego, merges thereby into the One Essence, to become not only one with "Us," the manifested universal Lives which are one Life, but that very Life itself.

THANK YOU FOR READING!

If you enjoyed this book, please consider leaving a review, even if it is only a line or two. It would make all the difference and would be very much appreciated.

Sign up for our newsletter to be the first to know when new books are published and receive a free bonus:

radiantbooks.co/bonus

ABOUT THE AUTHOR

Francia La Due (1849–1922) was born in the city of Chicago, Illinois. When she was four years old, her family moved to Syracuse, New York, where she spent most of her life until she moved to California. Even during her school years, La Due began to demonstrate exceptional literary talent. Later, she worked as a nurse despite having no medical education.

In 1894, La Due became a member of the Syracuse branch of the Theosophical Society, founded there in 1892 by Dr. William Dower. Together with Dower, she advocated for the rights of Native Americans. After the passing of Helena Blavatsky, the Great Brotherhood needed a new successor to continue its spiritual work in America. Thus, in 1898, the Master of Wisdom, known as Hilarion, began to guide La Due's activities. In the same year, she founded The Temple of the People in Syracuse.

However, the Master Hilarion later deemed it necessary to find a new location that would consider the intersections of the Earth's lines of force that create points of power. After two trips to California, La Due found an area on the eastern coast of the ocean. There, in 1903, she established the community of Halcyon, where a new stage of spiritual work of The Temple of the People started. La Due was the first head of the Temple, serving as its Guardian-in-Chief.

The Temple of the People published the monthly magazine *The Temple Artisan*, in which messages from the Master Hilarion, as well as from the Masters Morya and Koot Hoomi, were published for many years. The pages of this magazine also revealed a new section, *Theogenesis*, from the secret *Book of Dzyan*, which sheds light on the evolutionary path of humanity toward realizing its divine nature.

The members of the Temple succeeded in laying the foundation for scientific discoveries, such as microwave technology, the fruits of which are still bringing benefit to humanity today.

OTHER TITLES PUBLISHED BY RADIANT BOOKS

The Land of the Gods
by H. P. Blavatsky

HIDDEN in plain sight for 135 years, Blavatsky's story is a beautifully written account of an exceptional journey into Shambhala. Immersive and engaging, this profound book will provide you with a unique outlook on the deeper side of life, exposing our true nature, interior powers, and ultimate destiny. It explains grand, spiritual ideas more thoroughly and swiftly than any book you'll ever read.

The Book of the Golden Precepts
by H. P. Blavatsky

FULL of incomparable beauty and inspirational power, this book reveals the Secret Path to Enlightenment followed by the greatest spiritual teachers of all time, such as Jesus Christ and Gautama Buddha. If you're seeking real spiritual growth, if you long to access divine wisdom that will explain everything that is happening in the world, if you want to live with deeper and majestic purpose, this book is your key.

Revealing Cosmic Mysteries
by H. P. Blavatsky

LOST for over a century, the full stenographic reports of meetings with Blavatsky in London have resurfaced recently. Immerse yourself in those very meetings at which Blavatsky revealed secret knowledge. The questions others posed may well have been your own, and her answers will unlock your deeper understanding of the Universe's profound secrets. You will be privy to Blavatsky's inspirational power, brilliant and penetrating mind, sharp wit and authentic wisdom.

OTHER TITLES PUBLISHED BY RADIANT BOOKS

The Divine Government
by Helena Roerich

A SECRET for many years, this book provides the first-ever evidence showing how the Divine Government, known as *Shambhala*, helped the United States during the Franklin D. Roosevelt presidency. It outlines profound principles for becoming a true leader who can guide any nation to prosperity by building just relations between the people and the state.

The Temple of Mysteries
by Francia La Due

BRIDGING spirituality and science, this classic work is a true gem of the world's esoteric legacy. The Master Hilarion, the Protector of America and Europe, transmitted it through Francia La Due, intending to assist humanity in resolving the challenges of modern civilization and guide us toward unity with the cosmic forces that shape our existence. *The Temple of Mysteries* will illuminate your path to self-realization and help you find answers to the most pressing questions that trouble your soul.

The Mystery of Christ
by Thales of Argos

EYE-OPENING and heart-touching, *The Mystery of Christ* brings a fresh perspective, an uncommon insight, and spiritual depth to the dramatic events which occurred two thousand years ago. As you read the profoundly stirring pages of this beautifully crafted narrative, you will comprehend the unequalled mission of Christ and the innermost secrets of Mary, culminating in an unexpected encounter with the new mystery of the Cosmos named Sophia.

OTHER TITLES PUBLISHED BY RADIANT BOOKS

The Living Waters of Joy
by Grace Lucia Kimball

THROUGH heartfelt revelations, this book will become your sanctuary — a spiritual oasis where your troubled soul can always find comfort, peace, and renewal, even in the most difficult of times. Like a healing balm, its eloquent prose flows as a gentle stream of living water, offering you a profound and uplifting experience of the Higher Presence.

The Song of Sano Tarot
by Anna Fullwood

UNVEILING the fundamentals of creation, this book relates the story of Seven Forces, or vibratory laws, that govern your life and the entire Universe. Each of us belongs to a particular vibration, and if you do not live in accordance with your natural force, you will reap negative consequences. From this viewpoint, the book offers insights and practical advice on how to determine your inherent force and transform your life, thereby guiding you toward inner balance and peace.

Becoming What You Are
by Two Workers

DRAWING on timeless spiritual wisdom, this book will take you on a journey toward self-realization and inner awakening. Its inspiring messages and practical advice will show you how to cultivate the qualities necessary for spiritual growth. It will help you align your actions with your highest potential and ultimately become what you are — a radiant and awakened being.

OTHER TITLES PUBLISHED BY RADIANT BOOKS

The Seven Laws of Spiritual Purity
by Two Workers

Providing a profound and eye-opening perspective on achieving true spiritual purity, this thought-provoking and straightforward book draws practical advice from ancient wisdom to show you how to purify your mind, body, and soul. It is a passionate plea for a better world — a world in which humanity no longer has to accept and deal with the consequences of many sufferings but instead prevents their very causes.

The Kingdom of White Waters
by V.G.

For a thousand years, this secret story could be told only on the deathbed, for it revealed an inaccessible garden paradise hidden in the Himalayas — Shambhala, a place thousands of people searched for, but always failed to find. Each carrier of this secret story took a vow of silence that could be broken under only two conditions: when facing imminent death or in response to another's persistent requests for knowledge about the mythical Kingdom of White Waters.

www.ingramcontent.com/pod-product-compliance
Lightning Source LLC
Chambersburg PA
CBHW060607080526
44585CB00013B/724